THE
ENJOYMENT
OF MUSIC

This book by one of the best-known and most companionable of modern writers on music is an indispensible aid to the music-lover. Built round the known interests of a vast body of those for whom music is a chief recreation, and a catholic selection of some of the finest and most familiar of recorded masterpieces, it is designed to answer questions and to stimulate appreciation rather than to state theories. Drawing on his wide resources of scholarship in many fields Dr. Young provides a pattern of the aesthetics of music and of its historical development. The chapter headings show that all the main aspects of music, as they appear to the unprofessional but enthusiastic listener, are considered; but from a practical rather than from an academic point of view. While defining the essential differences between many types of music Dr. Young does so with deftness of touch and with a welcome economy of technical terminology.

THE
ENJOYMENT
OF MUSIC

Percy Young

THE ENJOYMENT OF MUSIC

AN EMI PUBLICATION

Published by E.M.I. Records,
20, Manchester Square, London W.1.

Made and Printed in Great Britain by
Hunt Barnard & Co. Ltd., Aylesbury, Bucks.

Front-cover photograph
by Anthony Lloyd-Parker

CONTENTS

FOREWORD

It seems almost unbelievable that the "enjoyment of music" has become the subject of a book.

Is it that we become progressively more keenly aware of joy as we isolate it and analyse the feeling – and then what happens to this dissected butterfly: does it lie dead in our hands and do we in fact, "understanding it", enjoy it the more?

How much does the Bushman read about the music he dances to, the music which sends him and us into a state of delirium, or, for that matter, how much did the ancient Athenian read about sculpture or the Russian about music and poetry?

Yet undeniably we must spend the little time left us in our ruthlessly scheduled lives reading about joy, deferring always the joy itself to a later date in the hope of "understanding" it and enjoying it still more.

Fortunately some people are not quite that self-denying, and even before they can dissect a symphony settle down of an evening to enjoy it – to cry or to laugh, with its changing humour and moods – as they would love their wives and children before "understanding" too much about them.

Or in loving do we not already understand more deeply, more justly than we might otherwise?

May this love never completely abandon our information – for only with love and sympathy do we keep our knowledge alive – otherwise it becomes less than useless – it becomes lethal.

Yehudi Menuhin

PREFACE

THE PUBLISHERS are conscious of an ever growing number of people interested in classical music through the medium of gramophone records. The ideal method of hearing music is of course to attend live musical events in various parts of the country; however for a number of reasons this is impossible for the majority of the population.

Outstanding efforts are made through radio and television in broadcasting a very wide range of music. If a musical composition has a great initial appeal to a listener with a consequent desire to hear the music again, it may be months or even years before the opportunity occurs. The gramophone record provides the means to hear such music as often as one requires.

There has been a continual striving for higher standards of sound reproduction and it has reached the point where the gap between reproduced sound and reality is very narrow, and this is particularly true of the higher standards of approximately the last decade. In their selection of records (listed at the back of this book) the Publishers have restricted their choice in the majority of cases to the world famous HMV and Columbia gold, red and dark blue labels – so that the reader has the benefit of recordings and performances of the highest artistic standards. Many of the world's leading artists are included for example: Klemperer, Barbirolli, Menuhin, Barenboim, Giulini, Los Angeles, Gedda, du Pré, Baker, to name just a few of EMI's exclusive artists.

We would stress that the reader should only be satisfied with the highest recording and artistic standards of musical works of art which will provide that additional enjoyment on repeated hearings over a protracted period of time.

It is a far cry from the crude cylinder machine of Thomas Edison in the late 1880's to the modern stereo equipment of

7

today, and yet Edison's chance discovery that sounds could be recorded and subsequently reproduced has provided the means of allowing the enjoyment of music in all homes. Edison conceived his discovery mainly in terms of a novelty and as a piece of office machinery.

Emil Berliner discerned the advantages of a flat disc as distinct from Edison's cylinder, and he also developed the technique of transferring the recorded sound on to "masters" and "stampers" from which thousands of records could be pressed. Berliner also saw the gramophone record as a source of home entertainment and the famous Caruso recordings of 1902 made by Fred Gaisberg (of the Gramophone Co. Ltd. – now part of EMI Ltd.) did much to help Berliner's conception to become a reality. The early recordings in the classical field were mainly of famous singers covering operatic arias and songs, and despite the noisy surfaces and the limited frequency range, the voice recorded surprisingly well. Orchestral recordings followed in 1913 but it was not until 1925 that the next major development was to take place in the history of the gramophone record.

Henry C. Harrison and Joseph P. Manfield developed the technique of recording sound electrically and this considerably widened the frequency range. As early as 1933 A. D. Blumlein, an EMI technician, had developed the process of making stereo recordings with two channels of sound pressed in a single groove of a record. However the lack of suitable raw material prevented this idea from becoming a reality until the late 1940's with the advent and growth of the plastics industry, and this made possible the long playing record. Whereas a single side of a record could only accommodate a mere 4½ or 5 minutes of music, the new type of record could offer around 25 minutes, and this has been extended, where necessary, to over half an hour. This meant that it was possible to hear, for example, a complete Mozart symphony or piano concerto on one side of a record, and compositions of almost an hour's duration on one record. Blumlein's conception of a stereo record became a reality in 1958. The two channels of sound are reproduced through two amplifiers contained in a single unit and two speaker units, and this gives the sound a greater ambience and a better "spread". It is well illustrated in listening to chamber music where two, three or four instruments are involved and the individual instruments can be located in the areas of sound issuing from the separate speakers. Naturally this adds to the realism and the actual enjoyment of the music. Furthermore it has to be appreciated that stereo offers a unique overall sound picture, with not only clarity of definition but also a richness and realism plus perspective and depth. Such qualities are not to be found on the normal single channel records, nor indeed on any of the so-called "transcribed" stereo discs currently in circulation.

The methods of reproducing sound have of course been closely associated with techniques of recording. There is now available a very wide range of reproducing equipment from a portable record player costing just over £10, to a highly sophisticated stereo equipment costing several hundred pounds. It is generally true that the greater cost of a particular product gives additional satisfaction and this is equally true of reproducing equipment and records. A cheap portable record player is obviously unsuitable for reproducing opera, but it is possible to purchase equipment costing between £75 to £100 which will give satisfactory stereophonic results in an average size lounge. However it is obvious that more expensive equipment will give greater satisfaction over many years. Modern stereo equipment is housed in attractively designed cabinets with the two speakers incorporated (or with separate speakers for the finest stereo results) to merge with many types of decor so that visual as well as aural demands are fulfilled.

I

The Enjoyment of Music

THERE is a story – at least half authentic – of a lady who once found herself in a state of distress. She went to her spiritual adviser and laid before him the cause of her distress. "Father," she said, "I no longer enjoy going to church." Never at a loss for words the priest observed: "My good woman, who ever told you that you *should* enjoy going to church." The anecdote has some relevance to the present case. Whether we enjoy music or not does not come under consideration until the question is put. In the beginning there is music. We are aware of music because – and this is increasingly the case – it is inescapable. And at some point someone asks: "Do you enjoy music?"

The question is, of course, indefensible. The answer, if given, merely adds one more to the ranks of the Davidites (those who consider themselves pro-music) or to those of the Philistines (anti-). If the direct answer is bad, the indirect answer is worse. Those who try the indirect answer put themselves at the mercy of the questioner. So – one person admits to a liking for "pop", and another for "classical". A third ventures into intellectual showmanship by confessing to a predilection for Baroque and an antipathy to Romantic. A fourth registers qualified approval of most music but draws the line firmly before anything that might be described as "modern". A fifth, usually in a particular age-group, advertises his with-it-ness by proclaiming for atonality and the aleatoric on the one hand, and the currently most publicised pop-group on the other – with nothing in between. The social phenomena here indicated are familiar, sometimes depressingly so, and it is worth the while of the quiet, undemonstrative, enthusiast to study their implications.

By doing so he (you) comes to certain conclusions about people and, by analysing what it is of and about, stands a good chance of increasing his enjoyment of music.

It depends – it is clear – on what is meant by enjoyment. The priest was right in one sense, and wrong in another. He was right in that he diagnosed a supineness in the pre-crisis nature of the lady's enjoyment; he was wrong in devaluing, or in appearing to devalue, the act of enjoyment. For this, broadly speaking, is what life is about. At once this puts music, as being a part of life, into a particular category, well away from the casual enquiry – "Do you enjoy music?"

The girl who was gyrating to the strains of the "group" threw a brief comment at her partner. She did not have to throw it far, but it overcarried and the world was the richer for: "It does something to you!" She spoke more profoundly than she knew (even though she laid no claim to philosophical originality). The basis of musical experience is that it does something to you.

At this point the smug attempt to opt out by making a virtue (highly prized by Philistines) of tone-deafness. Alas, short of total deafness – which is another matter, this is no more than a relative term, intelligible only within a defined area. Moralists are well aware that beat-music can drive the listener, more particularly a group of listeners, into a state of hysteria. In former times another kind of beat-music, in Spain, was reserved as a sovereign antidote against the poison of the tarantula spider. Hence the dance described as Tarantella.

The physical responses to music are many and varied. That they exist and are ineradicable is one point of departure for musician and music-lover alike. The self-styled music-hater, whose sole response is to fall asleep during the performance of 'classical" music (as he calls it) merely provides additional evidence: because this is the consequence of a chemical reaction he shows his first awareness by lapsing into a sometimes blessed unawareness. Maybe Shelley had this in mind when he described unheard melodies as sweeter than those that are heard.

It is well established that involvement with music tends on occasion to lead to tears. The classic tear-jerker – if the passing irreverence may be forgiven – is Handel's *Messiah*. One day in the autumn of 1759 – the year in which Handel died – a festival of his music took place in a village church in Leicestershire, England. The organiser of the festival, the vicar of the parish, wrote an account of the occasion. Regarding *Messiah* (which packed the church) he observed that nowhere was there a dry eye to be seen.

One day Tchaikovsky attended a concert in Moscow at which his first string Quartet (Op. 11) was being performed. He was sitting by Tolstoi, and that Tolstoi should have been seen to burst into tears during the slow movement convinced the composer that he had registered a signal success. As one who was prone to fits of weeping he could think of no greater compliment being paid to him. It made no odds to him that Tolstoi was notoriously unmusical in the normal way.

In part this kind of response is physical in origin. In part it is not. Emotional reactions to music are conditioned by an overlay of general experience. *Messiah*, for instance, was built into English experience as one vehicle by which sinners, urged to repentance, might travel in the general direction of virtue. This principle of belief was given an excellent start when the Dean of Downpatrick, at the first performance in Dublin, shouted to Mrs. Cibber, after her interpretation of "He was despised": "Woman, for this thy sins be forgiven thee".

A Dean who repeated Dr. Delany's behaviour today would, no doubt, be hauled off to a psychiatric ward. In the eighteenth century, however, emotional behaviour was more free – a circumstance to be borne in mind when music of that age is under closer review. Under certain conditions and in certain places, as described, an effusion of sentiment was not thought disgraceful in the nineteenth century.

So far we have shown that music exists and that an awareness of the fact of its existence leads to certain undeliberate and unconsidered consequences. What these are depends on a large variety of personal and social factors. One piece of music, however, is more than merely one piece of music. A Brandenburg Concerto by Bach, for example, was one thing to an eighteenth century audience in Brandenburg (if, indeed, the Court at

Brandenburg ever heard the concertos which are its chief memorial), another to a twentieth century audience at, say, the Bath Festival. It is still another thing to a non-European audience. More than this, each musical work lives a new and separate life within the secret confines of the imaginative perception of each individual listener.

There is a tendency to believe that a composition is both final and finite when it leaves the composer's pen. This is not really the case. The *idea* of any work is substantive, and definite in that it represents an artist's view of one aspect (or a unity of a variety of aspects) of human experience. But the exposition of the idea, which comes to us in the form of sonata, or symphony, or what you will, requires interpretation by the listener, who sieves it through the mesh of his own understanding, or capacity for appreciation. The outside observer – the critic, the scholar – can only be indirectly helpful. Either he gives an explanation of his own reactions, which is often supported by information relating to the history or structure of the particular work under review, or he contents himself with an accurate account of the work's external features and technical characteristics. Personalised criticism *par excellence* is that of Neville Cardus, while the analytical method is ideally demonstrated in the acute essays of Hans Keller. Criticism and scholarship are invaluable, but the listener must never feel himself obliged to deny the validity of his own conclusions.

There are stages in the development both of music itself, and of individual musical understanding. The way in which music has developed has been hinted at; in subsequent chapters the manner of its many-sided evolution will be shown in more detail. The consistent listener – the typical discophile, for instance – will realise how much the vision of music is enlarged by broadening experience. The man who listens to one work is able to say that he likes or dislikes it. He, however, who has listened to a hundred works is in a position to compare, and in so doing to discriminate, and even to judge. At this juncture he makes decisions. He goes to a concert, or turns on the radio, in order to hear something that he has deliberately selected. Or, of course, he does not go to a concert, or turns the radio off, in order to avoid hearing what he considers uncongenial.

Listening habits have been radically altered in the twentieth century. In former times one heard music in company (unless one played to oneself). One went to a concert, to an opera-house, into a church; and, because one was a member of a group, one's attitudes were to some extent conditioned by the group. After a virtuoso performance it was difficult to do other than applaud with becoming enthusiasm, simply because one's relationship to the performance through the group demanded it. To be a private listener in a public place is very difficult.

Composers knew this very well and the difference between one kind of music and another is, in fact, due to a recognition of environmental circumstances. The *Art of Fugue* was aimed at the single listener sealed in his own privacy; the Piano Concertos of Liszt, on the other hand, were aimed at the multitude. Bach played it cool; Liszt dropped a sensation into every ear. Now, however, we are in the position of having to adjust ourselves to frequent privacy, for mechanical reproduction makes it possible, for *private* listening to be rather more the rule than the exception. People go to concerts and recitals. Those who do mostly join with those who for various reasons do not or cannot, and comprise the great body of music-lovers whose appetite is generally nourished by musical performances that are mechanically reproduced.

The result is a new form of relationship. In public performance the intermediary, the interpreter – or group of interpreters – is seen. So far as recorded performance is concerned the interpreter remains unseen. In one sense the listener then is in direct contact with the creative mind of the composer. In another the performer, not being seen, acquires a new mystique. On the one hand there is, perhaps, a feeling of being face-to-face with genius; on the other a sense of circumambient magic. Altogether, the privacy of the experience tends to bring a refinement of experience.

For reasons which have already been hinted at – and which will be more fully explored – a form of magic has always been taken to be an attribute of music. More so than in respect of any other of the arts. There is something to be said in favour of coming into the field of musical experience at this point; to recognise at once the unworldliness of music. One would wish to begin to explore where music sounds like nothing but – music. In spite of the fact that it carries a title one might feel that Debussy's *La Mer* represented one of the outer limits of musical expression, being an issue of musical sounds that could only have been organised by a man who *thought* in musical terms.

The idea that music is a form of communication (it is even sometimes thought of as a special kind of language) is strongly held by some. If this notion is maintained it should be subject to the consideration that music is not a medium into which ideas otherwise expressible can be translated. *La Mer* is not a picture of a picture. It is a sequence of impressions first pinned down by the observer, and then released. We now come close to the abiding question: "What is it about?"

The pile of records grows. The enthusiast looks at them and contemplates their significance and the nature of his own sense of enjoyment. He begins to fashion his own critical and analytical guide. He begins to examine "the meaning of music".

If ever there was a 60 dollar question this is it: "What does he (the composer) mean?" Not unnaturally innumerable attempts have been made to supply answers. In fact a considerable industry has grown up around such attempts. The only valid answer is that which is supplied by the individual listener before he tries to formulate it in words.

On the way towards appreciation of music there are various staging-posts. The first is marked with the sign of the aesthete, to whom the best art is absolute, self-contained, and significant only as art. A vogue word of the school of Oscar Wilde was "exquisite". Exquisite music, in this sense, teased, tantalised, and titillated the sensations. For what it is worth, Wilde held Chopin, Schumann, and Dvořák in this class. At this stage, however, we might opt for Ravel as a master of the exquisite. Satiation of the senses by, say, the voluptuous instrumentation of *Daphnis and Chloë*, is not only possible but also probable. But this is not really the end of the matter. *Daphnis and Chloë* had another purpose. Being ballet music it was conceived as an expression of moods, actions, and even plot. It was music with a purpose. We may enjoy it as a self-contained experience or as a reflection of a series of enchanting actions on the stage, which we may have seen or which we may, when listening to the music, imagine we are seeing.

It may now be perceived that at one stage the term "knowledge" becomes effective, and the validity of the absolute aesthetic attitude diminishes. Musical experience expands our knowledge – but in its own unique way, and it is this uniqueness that is an important constituent in the pleasure dispensed. In itself a musical work conveys to the average listener (if we may presume that such a one exists) emotional attitudes, even emotional qualities, inherent in the personality of a particular individual – the composer. To this is added a secondary nexus of emotional involvements – of the performing artist. The composer, however, is as he is because of his environment. What we describe as "musical forms" are arrived at not merely through activities in a musician's workshop, but through the incidence of certain social and cultural events. A composer, then, is more than himself. To a greater or lesser extent he is a representative figure, exposing the spiritual, emotional, and even material conditions of a particular community at a particular time.

Enjoyment of music in the first place is prescribed by the senses. It is a mistake to resist this sort of pleasure. This, by the way, is a kind of warning against the earnest who suggest that total pleasure in an art can only be induced by an overlay of academic propriety. We should be quite clear about this. The most complete response to music comes by way of total surrender. I have no doubt that the process is virtually the same as falling in love, of which, according to Shakespeare, music is the proper diet. The analogy may, however, profitably be carried further. Falling in love with a person is one thing, living, either virtuously or unvirtuously, with that person is another. The initial accident provides the happy subject with some knowledge *of* his partner; the judicious follow-up supplements this with knowledge *about*. The latter is the basis of decision, and of long-term planning.

There are many to be found who having fallen in love with a musical work at first hearing have maintained a lifelong devotion. So far as I can remember my grandfather swore that there was only one piece of music – the "Hallelujah" chorus. Unmoved by the inescapable fact that Handel himself had composed at least half a dozen such choruses other than the famous I - saw - the - heavens - opened - and - the - great - God - Himself in *Messiah*, and being of a Puritan temperament, he held fast to musical monogamy. There are, perhaps, a dozen pieces of music (excluding hymns and national anthems, which have an in-built advantage) which have compelled the fidelity of thousands. These are the works that celebrities, as they are called, often propose for desert island consumption.

The desert island test is not a bad one to apply. Assuming oneself to be cast up with another person with whom one's emotions are spontaneously involved there are two possibilities: of endless delight, or, after the wearing-off of the first, fine, careless, rapture, of interminable boredom. Love at first sight is vulnerable after re-scrutiny. While recognising the validity of the initial enthusiasm aroused by music, I am obliged to lean on the psychological truism just expressed and to advise a certain prudence. He (or she) who buys a recording does so in most cases because he (or she) looks forward to an indissoluble union. Such a union is helped by a certain amount of previous knowledge about the object in question.

Let us return to the broad question of the composer as a representative figure. Two of the most significant works ever composed in the tradition, and according to the conventions, of Western European music are Bach's *St. Matthew Passion* and Beethoven's "Eroica" Symphony.

There is no doubt that very many music-lovers are at once overwhelmed by both works, either in part or as a whole. In both cases, however, the first emotional reaction is succeeded by a feeling of incompleteness. What is the meaning of *Passion* on the one hand, and of "Eroica" on the other? Both works are avowedly more than musical experiences, because the text of the one and the implicit narrative, or programme, of the other, so inform us. And if the total of the experiences intended by the composers is greater than a purely musical experience in order to embrace the total experience we must be prepared to push beyond the musical frontiers.

The theme of the *St. Matthew Passion* is that of tragedy. According to Christian teaching, to which Bach was strictly obedient, the tragedy is of god-size dimension. But the tragedy of the god is also the tragedy of man – since, theologically speaking, the god became man. The tragedy of man, however, is the tragedy of men. At once we sense a relevance to our own general experience. The way in which Bach shaped his thoughts was in part, at least, due to the succession of tragic events that had taken place in his country during the two centuries that elapsed between the lives of Martin Luther and J. S. Bach. The central feature of the *St. Matthew Passion* is the chorale, and the chorale for the people of Lutheran Germany was a symbol both of the struggle for religious independence and the potential of national unity. The place of music of the type of the *Passion* was written into the German tradition through years of privation and destruction. The character of Bach's music was the outcome of the experiences of the wars of the sixteenth and seventeenth centuries, and particularly of the Thirty Years War.

The "Eroica" Symphony is also tragic on the grand scale. This, however, is the exposition of the tragedy not of a god who became man and involved himself in the conflict of the world, but of a man who aspired to become a god. Such is implicit in the term heroic – a term out of fashion in the second half of the twentieth century. Beethoven stood at a cross-roads in history. Behind him lay the record of feudal, absolutist, governments, that fenced in the natural aspirations of men towards at least freedom of thought. Before him lay a future in which humanity would, through the triumph of reason and justice, prevail over the autocracy of autocrats. For Beethoven the symbol of emancipation was the First Consul. But Napoleon tore up his ideals and became an Emperor, so Beethoven tore up the dedication of his Third Symphony, and left the heroic theme in the abstract.

These last paragraphs put two works within contexts. The

works thus take on a wider significance – and so does music as a whole. Now the knowledge about these particular works conveyed in this philosophical-historical manner does appear to me to enhance their already existing emotional importance in the mind of the listener. The information so far from detracting from the force of the initial response, that we may presume to have been created by the act of listening, increases it. For many aspects of the emotional background to the particular works are, in broad terms, exposed.

In listening to music, whether we like it or not, the subconscious is involved; in composing music the subconscious is also involved. The common denominator is the total of common and communal experience that is enveloped in the general subconscious. At this point the actual date at which a work of art was created becomes irrelevant, for the subconscious is independent of time. This goes some way to explaining why what was composed two or three hundred years ago is still affective.

The communicative value of music may be ignored, but it can hardly be denied. Appreciation of what is communicated is naturally linked with appreciation of how communication is effected. This is a matter of style. At some stages in social development style is taken to be more important than at others. Or rather, there are different emphases at different periods. In the eighteenth century the style in which a letter was written mattered; in the twentieth century writing letters has given way before the onslaught of the telephone. But even so, he who telephones with a due respect for style is likely to get a more satisfactory reaction than he who does not. Style is not, as may sometimes be suggested, artifice; it is art. In short it is the selection of the right tools for the job. Often these tools are to hand, but sometimes new tools needs to be invented.

The raw material of music lies in the sounds of voices and of instruments. The composer uses both as they exist within his experience and environment. We may go back to the Bach and Beethoven examples. Bach used two choirs in the *St. Matthew Passion*, because he had two choirs at his disposal in St. Thomas's School, Leipzig. (In fact he could have used three or four choirs if he had so wished, but had he done so he would have run into logistical complications.) Also, there was a hundred-year-old tradition of using double choir in German religious music. He used strings, harpsichord, organ, flutes, various kinds of oboes, and bassoons, as the basis of his orchestra. These resources were available to him, and beyond them he could not go.

In the "Eroica" Symphony the orchestra includes clarinets in a woodwind section that has gained a high degree of independence, and a potent force of trumpets and horns, which together with the drums, add a new dimension. In the way in which the two composers handle these multiple resources we become aware of one element of style. These stylistic details are seen at once to be integral to the whole matter of communication.

The *St. Matthew Passion* occupies nine sides of long-playing discs. The "Eroica", on the other hand, requires only two. The time factor also has an effect on style. Composers may sometimes appear to be, and sometimes are, arbitrary in the matter of length; but on the whole the dimension of a work is dictated by social custom. As a provider of material to occupy a certain period of time the composer needs to adjust his thinking to the time available. If an audience for a particular purpose requires two minutes of music (as may be the case either under the limitations imposed by a specific part of a liturgy or by a radio, television, or film producer) the composer must gear himself to economy. If, on the other hand, he is given a two hour stretch (less likely now than formerly, except in the field of opera) he can take a more leisurely and more expansive line. He may, to use the technical term, "develop" his ideas.

The gap between the extremes of economy and extravagance is filled by a number of structural devices which are called musical "forms". Musical forms have changed from time to time, not because someone or other has decided that the time is ripe for change for the sake of change, but because of altered attitudes towards the general factor of time. Forms, however, stand for more than this. They were also the answer to inclinations to emphasise one or other of the tendencies inherent in the nature of musical expression. The point to understand is that "form" is not to be understood in isolation. It is, of course, helpful for a would-be composer to read a dissertation on the techniques of fugal writing, or on the mechanics of serial composition. I doubt whether such literature is entirely helpful to the reader for whom this book is written. One has an awareness of the frustrations imposed on the hopeful by well-meaning, but misdirected, efforts of generations of pedagogues for whom the set patterns revealed by musical pathologists were a ready help in times of trouble.

What we conclude is that music lives, organically. The enjoyment of music depends entirely on the acceptance of this living quality. Paradoxically the facts of modern musical dissemination enable one to appreciate the living quality of music more rather than less.

Sitting alone (or in congenial and familiar company) one can, so to speak, be face to face with Bach, Beethoven, Mozart, Mendelssohn, Schubert, Schumann, Strauss. . . . The music that one selects for pleasure becomes a solace in isolation, a fulfilment of aspiration, a guide to virtuous or unvirtuous living; at any rate, a complement to self. This agreed we then must allow the present companionship and existence of the first cause of the music: the composer, and his aides, the performers. This, on the whole, is what is meant when music is described as immortal.

The enjoyment of anything has many facets. In a flippant mood somewhat earlier I had the temerity to join together both sacred and profane love; not because of any stronger than normal inclinations to pagan thought, but because the division between the two is unwholesome. The one is the obverse of the other. Either way, however, there is certain interest in the matter of vital statistics. It will be agreed that on the one hand this may be described as human interest. In the succeeding chapters I hope that the vital statistics on the other side may also be shown to possess human interest.

2

Musical Structures

THERE is an idea that perception of artistic values and appreciation of art depends on the possession of particular virtues, or the acquisition of special skills. This idea was nourished particularly during the period of the Renaissance, the period which elevated the "man of taste" to a pinnacle of self-esteem from which he has been more or less finally and unceremoniously deposed during the last twenty or so years. The ideal of the "man of taste" – derived from conceptions of aristocracy that have also lost validity – was zealously cultivated within the educational system of Britain. In due course the arts, and particularly that of music, were made to play their part in promoting tastefulness. The aim was not so much to know the arts, as to know about them; to be able to discuss them. Now this is where we meet the first difficulty. What do we discuss?

The other day I met a man generally considered knowledgeable in such matters on my way to a concert, and the frequent inability of people to get on the right wave-length was borne in on me when he observed that Liszt was not much of a hand at "development". The remark was à propos of the First Piano Concerto which we were on our way to hear. At that moment I was not in the mood for analytical disputation. I wanted to hear this work of Liszt – not in bits, shredded out under the pseudo-scientist's microscope, but in all its full-bloodedness. It so happened that within two days of that adventure I encountered a fourteen-year-old schoolgirl, earnest in her musical endeavours, and keen to protect the security of her teacher's employment. She was on her way to solitude to write an essay on the history of "thematic metamorphosis" between 1830 and

23

1890 (or thereabouts). Now, whatever this occupation may do towards inculcating notions of rectitude in the field of musical education its effect on appreciation, as I understand it, is minimal.

The solitary listener attached only to his/her record-player or radio, is in a happier position. He is neither expected to discuss "development" nor the "metamorphosis of themes". On the other hand, while passionately devoted to the relationship established between himself and the creative agent (composer, composer *plus* poet or librettist, or both *plus* performers) he may well feel a need to define the terms of their relationship. To do this he is helped somewhat by knowing something of the intention within the idea of the specific work and the means whereby the intention has been fulfilled. There are thus two avenues to be explored. In the long run one explores both. Indeed eventually one learns to explore both at the same time. In the first place, however, one chooses one of the two for immediate investigation. Which one depends on conformations and structure of personality. The word structure is here significant.

The structure of personality has fascinated poets and exercised the minds of priests, doctors, and psychologists, more or less from the beginning of time. In general, it has been convenient to see personality in two complementary and contrasting sections, which have been, and continue to be, given labels of convenience. Within the context of the arts we hear sometimes of the antithesis between Appolonian and Dionysian – or between classical and romantic – attributes. In absolute terms the classical mind, working inductively, establishes coherence and significance of pattern from what is, or what is taken to be, real. The romantic mind, apprehending or assuming the existence of a general, abstract, ideal, works deductively from that ideal. At some point – in the arts at all events – the real and the unreal, the objective and the subjective, the classical and the romantic, meet. It is at this point of meeting that one encounters those forms of artistic expression that seem to have the widest influence. Which is, of course, only to say that the two aspects of art which co-exist have become complementary.

One has a natural tendency to structuralise one's perception according to the patterning of one's own personality. The natural romantic summarises his responses by the use of evocative terms. The most common of such terms is "beautiful" (which has many variants, but all expressing somewhat similar reactions). This is a term with many shades of meaning, each of which only means what it means to the person who uses it. It is splendid, but vague. How vague may be most readily understood by letting it loose in respect of a particular film-star (or model) in a cinema- or photo-phile company. "Beautiful" is a term to be taken up with reserve; it carries one beyond the frontiers of belief.

One may, I suppose, say that the "Jupiter" Symphony of Mozart is beautiful. But having said it one has said nothing. For the non-romantic may legitimately reply that if it is then he can't accept "beautiful" as valid of definition. On the other hand a non-romantic – or one whose romantic tendencies are strictly controlled – may, having heard the same work observe that it is well-made, well-proportioned, balanced, and so on. Such observations on the "Jupiter" are not only true within their context, but also susceptible of proof. They rest on solid foundations of fact. There are four movements united by tonality, each programmed (in the computer sense) according to basic thematic material, and held within definable limits of sonorities and timbres.

Now the classical view (taking classical in its broad and not its restricted sense) can be so cogently presented that we may be all but persuaded that we are missing something if we do not manage to keep in touch with the time-table of events that constitute the form of the work. Hence the schoolgirl chasing her metamorphosed themes to make a pedant's holiday. Yet, at the same time we know that the classical, analytical, attitude is insufficient. The "Jupiter" Symphony is more than the sum of its parts, and we are brought back to consideration of what for want of a better term we call the "spirit" of the music – its personality.

This is where we return to the matter of intention. To know something about a composer's intention helps somewhat to understanding the structure of his personality and the structure of the personality of his music. In the "Clock" Symphony (No. 101) and the "Farewell" Symphony (No. 45) of Haydn we are permitted to refer to the composer's humour in respect of the slow movements of the former and the finale of the latter. The orchestral introduction to *The Creation* is legitimately to be described as exploratory, since it covers areas of musical experience previously not examined in quite that way by that composer. The Fifth Symphony of Beethoven goes in one direction, the Sixth – quite contrasting – goes in another. And so we may go on to note that each worth while work has its own labelled peg on which to hang.

These pegs, and their labels, are solely useful for the sorting-out of the personality structures of music. Sometimes we are instructed, by one or another, as to what we should recognise; sometimes, however, we are left to arrive at our own conclusions. Where music is allied with words – as in song, oratorio, or opera – the words are (or should be) the clue to recognition. In programmatic music, i.e. where a specific indication as to intention is available through title – i.e. *Sinfonia Antartica* (Vaughan Williams) – or through explanatory essay – as in the case of Berlioz's *Symphonie Fantastique* – then we have a general statement of intent. All this is on the side of romanticism. Where, however, all we start with is a bald classification such as Symphony No. 3, in F major (Brahms) we are left to draw our own conclusions.

Nonetheless in all cases we are left in no doubt that music, representing conflicts of ideas (patterns of sounds which are only significant in relation to one another or of ideals translated into states of emotion or mood), is a complex of patterns which form into individual structures bounded at the extremes, and sometimes punctuated, by silence. The structure of human personality is what exists between birth and death, the points of emergence from and return to oblivion. In this way a musical work, which grows out of and ultimately gets lost in oblivion, holds a certain symbolism of which the listener is unconsciously aware. This is a first cause for the apparent necessity of music, and for its social significance.

The "Jupiter" Symphony is in the key of C major. The First Symphony of Beethoven is in C major. Both works, composed within the last dozen years of the eighteenth century, and within the so-called "classical period", use the same kind of instruments and follow the same general ground-plan, or "form". But the differences between these two works are more than the similarities. Each work as we hear it, is an individual experience not to be encountered in any other way. Each work, in fact, has its own, unique overall structure, which is more important than the mere plan, or form, employed to maintain the structure.

The point has been made at some length because it is fundamental. If it is not appreciated then the earnest soul in search of spiritual enrichment by way of musical experience will get entangled in an undergrowth of technicalities.

One should, however, not fail to observe that technicalities have their own separate attraction. In the *Variations on a theme of Haydn* Brahms looks at a not very distinguished, albeit not unattractive, tune from a wind-band divertimento probably composed by Ignaz Pleyel and not by Haydn, and then having mentally reduced it to its basic elements reassembles those elements into new shapes. Of these some are distinguished by their texture, some by their harmonic coloration, some by their rhythmic energy, some by their combination of linear aspects into contrapuntal conclusions. There comes the point when one wonders how it is done. Here one goes back to the man making his music. In making his music the composer, from experience, envisages a set of structures within a structure.

The composer begins where we end. He has in mind at the outset the whole work – at least as a general impression – for the evolution and ultimate definition of which he uses various techniques. At some point the composer has consciously learned these techniques. At the stage of composition, matured by experience, he uses the techniques without much conscious thought. This process is often miscalled inspiration.

Music, passing in time, is insubstantial. Its very insubstantiality is one of its attractions, for it is this quality that acts as antidote to many of the problems of the listener's environ-

27

ment. The unreality of music, however, affects the listener, particularly the casual listener, more than the composer. He, for whom music is the first and most natural form of expression, is a realist for whom the substance of music is reality. Some composers are more realist than others – contrasting, for example, the highly professional Mendelssohn with his friend and contemporary, Schumann – but all are concerned with the manipulation of acoustical phenomena that have physical existence.

Music is ideas; more palpably it is sound. And what immediately signifies is the transmission of sound. In the first place this depends on medium. Music is created in a physical sense by instruments (the voice being in this instance one kind of instrument), and the instrument or instruments used in any particular work impose their own structural conditions. Of this, contemporary music makes us increasingly aware.

Music exists in time, but in so far as our awareness of it goes it also exists in space. That is to say, the singers in a choir are placed here and there in self-contained groups, as also are the performers in chamber or orchestral music. At one period the illusion that in any kind of corporate music-making there should only be one broad, homogeneous, mass of tone was built up. Hence the kind of tone evoked from the huge symphony orchestra, or choir, of nineteenth century proportions and disposition. The rediscovery of the effects produced by situation is one of the more exciting aspects of contemporary music. This is readily appreciable through the development of stereophonic techniques in reproduction. It may now be heard that music has its left and its right, its north and its south, and that second violins are not merely inferior first violins. In the music of John Cage or Karlheinz Stockhausen we find ourselves surrounded by sound effects, which no longer emerge from one, but from different sources. There is, of course, a lot more to it than this (and the music of Stockhausen lies outside this scrutiny); but that the position of the musicians (or loudspeakers disseminating effects on tape) is an effective factor in the formation of music is acknowledged by Stockhausen in his application of the term "structural procedures" to describe the condition of his *Gruppen* – a work for 3 orchestras.

A good deal of music has been partly conditioned by the properties of architecture. Venetian and Bolognese composers of the sixteenth and seventeenth centuries exploited the possibilities of choral and/or instrumental groups placed in separate galleries, just as English composers made use of the facing stalls in the choirs of cathedrals and churches. The outcome of such antiphonal effects was the structuralisation of music so that a complex form of antiphony was built into the approach of the composer to the material of music. At the same time the audience hearing music, for instance, by Giovanni Gabrieli, the great late Renaissance master of Venetian music appreciated (without having to analyse) the structural propriety of antiphonal music whether of voices, or instruments, or both. In a classical piano concerto the antithesis between the solo instrument and the group is a major source of the pleasure derived from the concerto, and the manner in which the music is laid out depends on those antiphonal techniques effectively brought into musical composition during the Renaissance period.

Allied to the antiphonal principle is that of the exploitation of echo. Echo, so to speak, exists before music exists but the incorporation of the phenomenon of echo into musical structure is responsible for multi-dimensional development of sound-effects. Echo is repetition, and the foundation of extended thematic statement is repetition of material. Until the twentieth century the processes of music have been almost entirely constructed into viable patterns by means of repetition. But echo is also a phenomenon that has dynamic force, with the *plus* of loud and the *minus* of soft. It is doubtful whether the structure of a work can be grasped without a perception of its dynamic properties, which – between the extremes of Tchaikovsky's *pppp* and *fff* – form another of the inner structures of music. This opens up fascinating possibilities, for it is within a range of appropriate dynamics that a performing artist, or a conductor, has most discretion. Interpretation then depends on the kind of structure evolved by the performer within the dynamic field.

Some buildings are acoustically more alive than others.

Churches tend to be resonant, and the factor of resonance qualifies both sonority and speed. The former is enhanced by ample resonance, while, on the other hand, high speeds are made hazardous. The salon, which was the first home of purely instrumental music, lacked the mystical associations created by the resounding vaults of ecclesiastical architecture, and gave opportunity for quicker tempi and groupings of quicker notes, to be undertaken with little danger to the clarity of the musical texture. On the whole the details of argument that characterise post-Renaissance music owe a good deal to the fact of the congeniality or otherwise of acoustical environments. One of the problems (and there are many) of dealing with what generically is termed early music is that of accommodating present-day performance to the right kind of acoustical setting.

Ideally a variety of auditoriums are required in any musical centre for the proper reproduction of works of different periods. In the public sense this is impracticable, and one normally makes do with the multi-purpose concert hall (often built with the conditions of the nineteenth century "symphony orchestra" in mind). In this respect it is clear that in recording music there is opportunity to take into account the not unimportant matter of acoustical environment. The point is understood when listening to an organ recital or to polyphonic choral music played and sung under church or cathedral conditions. There is, it may be added, a virtue in showing relevant architectural features on record sleeves, for these can have a powerful evocative influence on the appreciative faculties of the imaginative listener.

So far, then, we have a broad, not very closely defined area of a musical work. In the exposition of an idea the composer is affected to a considerable extent by the circumstances of performance; and these show in one way or another in the lay-out of the music.

There now comes the necessity for considering in a more detailed way how the idea, already somewhat structuralised by environment, is to be given coherence.

Composition is largely a matter of selection and rejection. Theoretically there is no reason why one should not string together sounds in a purely arbitrary manner. Despite protestations to the contrary there may well be a suspicion that this is the main achievement of contemporary *avant-garde* movements. For all I know the concatenation of acoustical accidents that passes into the mythology of the twentieth century as aleatoric musical experience may be what composers have been wanting to do for centuries. Somehow, however, I have a feeling that this was not the direction in which they were looking. The main tradition of western music (and a good deal of oriental music) has been concerned with uniting the particles of music into units that added up to some kind of sense rather than mere non-sense.

In the past the composer and the audience were at one in regarding the elements of musical experience as melody, a system of varied but related pitches controlled by rhythm; the manifold expansion of melodic gestures into textures described as harmony or counterpoint (the two often come so close together that it is not possible to speak of the one without taking into account the other); and instrumentation. Supposing we have a string quartet – 2 violins, a viola, and a cello. Most of the time during the performance of a work written for this medium we are conscious of melodic ideas which may from time to time emanate from any one of the instruments. Sometimes we distinctly hear, or apprehend, a combination of two or more simultaneous tunes. At other times while three of the instruments are active we are aware that the fourth is enjoying the limelight. Throughout the performance attention is stimulated by different qualities of tone-colour.

In that continuity is the first essential to musical coherence we depend on the existence of melody, which if it is not continuous is not recognisable as melody, to guide our enquiries into the nature of the particular music to which we are listening. The ultimate structuralisation of music within the general repertoire arises from the behaviour of sounds of recognisable thematic extraction within thematic contexts.

Theme is not quite melody. A theme may be a suggestion towards a melody. It is open-ended. A melody is end-stopped. A theme is not necessarily self-important; a melody normally is.

This is the point at which understanding of the *art* of music – as distinct from an appreciation of music – begins.

A melody registers at once (that is when it is accepted by the listener as completed); the significance of the behaviour of a theme becomes apparent only after consideration not only of what has happened to it but also of what might have happened to it. What is generally, and not improperly, described as "popular" music is primarily melodic: this applies from folk-songs and ballads of whatever age and origin, by way of such hardy annuals from the classics as the "Air on the G string" and Handel's so-called "Largo" to today's "top of the pops". There are, of course, differences of attitude towards inessentials but fundamentally there is an appreciable unity which is defined by the limits of, and limitations on, melodic contour.

We accept a melody as it is and for what it is. At the same time the fact of its organisation is not to be ignored, and, although we may not consciously analyse its organisation we are at least unconsciously aware of it. It is inevitable that a popular melody owes its popularity in large measure to the ease with which it can be held in the memory and also repeated.

A viable melody lives within a tonal area. That is, we describe it as being within a specific mode (if it antedates the classical key system) or a specific key (major or minor). In either case the melody is distinguished by the primacy of certain sounds, the most important of which is the "tonic" (1st note of the scale), and the second most important is the "dominant" (5th note of the scale). A melody, its origins in word formations and, frequently, the practice of lyric poetry, is a statement which, for the sake of clarity, is sectionalised. It appears, therefore, as a sequence of phrases. Memorability being basic to melodic intention the constituent phrases are inter-related. Some are directly repeated. In other cases rhythmic patterns are maintained below changes of contour. What comes out as simplicity itself is, indeed, fairly far from absolute simplicity. It is accepted that among composers none is more spontaneous than Franz Schubert, and of all his songs that are in the popular repertoire none would seem to be more artless than the setting of Goethe's *Heidenröslein.*

32

This is a 3-stanza song, with the same music for each stanza. (The setting, therefore, is termed "strophic"). There is, then, one melody three times repeated. We hear this melody, and accept it as a total experience. Yet if listened to a second time, with attention paid to the sections rather than to the whole, it will be noticed that a crystalline formation of some complexity becomes apparent. The melody is pegged down between the highest and the lowest notes of the major scale, and it will be appreciated that the placing of these notes is one important factor in the personality shape of the melody. It will also be appreciated that the first four notes – the same note repeated – are the motivation of subsequent rhythmic activity. The first phrase (the melody to the first line of poetry) is repeated for the third phrase; but with a difference. One note is marginally altered; and this alteration produces a climatic change. In musical terms the key is changed. The fact is less important than the impression created by this change. Of the impression the listener is unconsciously aware; in respect of the fact the consciousness must be invoked. Whether knowledge of the fact adds to enjoyment is doubtful. But it does enhance appreciation – of the subtleties that underly the essential simplicities of the creative operation.

It is, I think, important to bear in mind that a composer is not a critic, nor is he a musicologist. In respect of creation – and this obtains in all branches of art – the creative mind is concerned in the first place with simple issues. If it were not so the prolificacy of the greatest artists would have been impossible. The artist envisages a complete work, which represents a whole idea. His starting-point is a minimal stock of raw materials. The taste of composition is to utilise the raw materials in such a way that in due course they embrace the general idea.

In respect of music this means profitable occupation of a time continuum. The manner in which this occupation is accomplished depends on a number of conditions; on available resources, on function, and on environment.

The main structures of music have grown out of circumstance, and thus should not be considered as independent and isolated phenomena. This will be more fully explained in subsequent chapters. Here we may consider some basic principles relating to certain processes of thematic extension.

It has already been seen that within melody the principle of repetition is fundamental. It has also been indicated that repetition also involves variation. Variation, of course, may be merely one of expression. That is to say, a performer (either under instruction from the composer or acting on his own initiative) can vary the dynamic of a phrase that is repeated, and in so doing give it additional significance. Variation may be more or less embellishment, as in Handel's so-called "Harmonious Blacksmith"; in which case the interest of the observer is in superficialities. Or variation, as in the instance of the inflected phrase in *Heidenröslein*, may be of some fundamental importance within the structure of the music. In the final issue the coherence of what in broad terms is accepted as classical music depended a great deal on the variation principal so modified as to be free to expand.

In the Middle Ages the basic material of art music was the liturgical melody. For theological and doctrinal reasons the liturgical melody was an absolute necessity. The medieval and Renaissance composer, therefore, was compelled to design around set formulae. The medieval and Renaissance attitude to musical structuralization was accordingly conditioned by the necessity of retaining a particular thematic shape in a reasonably conspicuous position. The set tune was placed in the tenor voice, with other voices surrounding it with complementary and contrasting lines of sound. Or the melody was shifted from part to part, the process of setting it off against other melodic lines being maintained.

At a second stage the originating melody was fragmentated, with segments only being shown. At this stage a thematic *incipit* in one part inspired other parts to follow suit. Thus, in sixteenth century music, the imitation of one voice by another became an accepted feature. The principle was taken over by instrumental music, and its extension led to the evolution of the fugal manner of design. A fugue is monothematic in that it is based on patterns evolved from, or designed to contrast with, a set theme. The theme of a fugue, known as the "subject", is

34

delivered in isolation and then worked into a network of instrumental or vocal parts. However complex the texture, and however involved the argument, the one initial theme (often not important or significant in itself) is supreme, as is to be readily appreciated from, say, the fugue of Bach's Toccata and Fugue in D minor.

Because it has occupied a great deal of academic attention it has often been erroneously assumed that the form of fugue is the culmination of musically scientific achievement. The status of fugue has been largely maintained by the respect held for Bach's *Well-Tempered Clavier*. A half-hour of listening is sufficient to assure oneself that the marvel of these works lie not in the mastery of form evinced but in the poetical and dramatic ideas that are conveyed. There is, it should be noted, no uniformity of structure. A general principle obtains, which was a lever to invention and original observation. Fugue came down from the Middle Ages to the present day (e.g. Britten's fine conclusion to the *Young Person's Guide to the Orchestra*) and crosses over all schools and fashions. Which suggests that, so far from being the strictest of tyrants, it is, to the composer in general, the most congenial of companions.

Other methods of monothematic extension were evolved in the crucial period of the Renaissance. At this time the influence of secular music began to be infectious, and the development of instrumental music was made easier by a fusion of techniques. Strophic repetition was a feature of song, but also of dance. It was from the latter that the principle of "ground bass" was derived. *Chaconne* and *Passacaglia*, which formally indicate a continually repeating motiv in the bass part, were indeed the names of dances. As in the case of fugue the theme of a work in *chaconne* or *passacaglia* form is not important except in so far as it awakens the imagination of the composer. That the structure need not be inhibiting may be recognised by comparing the Chaconne from Purcell's *King Arthur* with Bach's C minor Passacaglia (and Fugue) for Organ, and both with the final movements of Brahms's Fourth and Vaughan Williams's Fifth Symphonies.

Forms such as fugue and ground bass are classified as contrapuntal, the distinguishing feature being the simultaneity of inter-related thematic statements. Allied to fugue (which has correlative terms such as *ricercare* and *canzona*, according to place of origin) are canons and rounds, both of which are rather stricter and more circumscribed than fugue. Canonic style is more frequent than pure canon in extended works. It is to be found throughout the music of Bach (whose reputation in his own day was that of a musical scientist), particularly in chorale preludes for organ, and such virtuoso feats of musical organisation as the "Goldberg" Variations and the Art of Fugue. But the contrapuntal tradition of which fugue, canon, and so on, are part, has remained central to all constructive musical thinking and is to be noticed in such latter-day composers as Mendelssohn, Schumann, Brahms, Reger, Schoenberg, Hindemith, Vaughan Williams, *et al*.

On the whole it may be said that the exigencies of contrapuntal structures tend to draw the composer to statements inspired by a sense of resolution and seriousness. The attitude is one of the many that is built into musical experience because of past associations. Thus the fact that Beethoven's *Grosse Fuge* is a fugue attaches to it a bonus mark from the start.

A structure in itself, however, is neutral. It is what use is made of it that counts.

Contrapuntal music represents one aspect of musical invention, and relies on development in depth. That is to say, thematic interest is not confined to the top part, but is distributed more or less equally between all parts.

It is clear that lateral development is possible, and this has already been shown in respect of the nature of melody, and the repetition of melody in that most congenial of patterns – "air and variations". The latter, of which there are innumerable examples, is congenial to the listener who is seldom taken far away from sight of land.

In the seventeenth century the voice, formerly primarily considered as a vehicle for words-with-music, was up-graded to the status of an instrument, and was treated as such. The outcome of this new approach was the division of singing music into *recitative* (in which the word-message was given priority) and the *aria* (in which the potential of the voice was exploited within a generous and expansive scheme). This scheme was tripartite: a first section, a second section of contrasted character and disposed within a new, but related, tonal climate, and a final section which repeated the first, but with added embellishments. The matter of the Baroque aria was extended by related instrumental passages, or *ritornelli*.

During the Baroque era various facets of musical thought and activity began to come together into a new unity of approach and expression. The former supremacy of sacred art music was reduced, with the result that instruments came into their own while the lead in vocal techniques came not from the church but, the opera house. The status that music had enjoyed in medieval philosophy was transferred to the wider philosophies inspired by the Renaissance. In the so-called Age of Reason music was a vital element in social life on every level, and although primarily under aristocratic patronage, it was cohesive. The emotional qualities inherent in the art were symbolised in the two-theme contrast of the sonata form that emerged somewhere about the middle of the eighteenth century. The scientific properties and the logical potential attached to music were exposed in the proportioning of sonata structures according to a scheme of relationships between tonalities. The symbol of the classical age was the symphony – in which dance (minuet and rondo particularly) and song (in the aria type slow movement that prevailed) were combined with the rhetoric and argument that constituted the important first movement design in itself defined as "Sonata form".

The symphony, therefore, was a compendium of musical structures, and so it has remained. It is for this reason that the collective term has remained as a useful cover for large-scale operations. However, the famous symphonies of Haydn, Mozart, and Beethoven, were regarded as excellent music not because they were symphonies but because they were good symphonies – i.e. good music. The point should not be lost on the enthusiast who is concerned lest he has too little "knowledge about". It is the "knowledge of" that matters.

At the same time a strong structural sense, representing a

sense of order, is a necessity to the composer, who, by observation of a certain code is obliged to condense his material and to give it coherence. The formal structures, or forms, of music grew up as part of the courtesies of expression. At the very least by knowing what general form is being used the listener knows what to exclude from consideration. One does not, for example, look for the "tune" in a fugue.

In former times, in its own way, music was functional; as vital to social organisation as the other arts and sciences. The old structures were symbolic of this functionalism, and they began to be devalued and replaced when function mattered less than formerly. In the nineteenth century music moved over from a fairly central position into the growing field of inessential, but none the less desirable, attractions. The crisis of musical structures, illustrated by the break-down of the system of tonal security, occurred when music became of more interest on account of what it was, than what function it served.

There is no better starting-point for a survey of the significance of functionalism than the Renaissance–Baroque period, in which the creative musician was less esteemed for his creativity than for his prolificacy or his due regard for delivering material on time, and, it may be added, in time.

3

Renaissance and Baroque

ONE is liable to be swept up by current fashion. The critic, following the lead of the musicologist, who now exercises a strong influence on listening habits, shouts "Renaissance" and there is a scurry in that direction; or he cries "Baroque", and the music clubs become Baroque-conscious. In the first place we absorb anything from Francesco Landino (the friend of Dante) to Orlando di Lasso; in the second anything from Monteverdi to Telemann. Apart from the fact (that should not be unexpected) that there is always more music unknown than known, the operation is often executed as a gesture of despair; as a rejection of contemporary values and as part of the quest for an always mythical "golden age".

The tendency to look back under the impression that the present is a write-off is to be resisted. Under scrutiny, any sector of human activity, at any time, shows more depressing than encouraging aspects. The surviving works of art (in the case of music, survival is fortuitous) represent attempts, on the one hand to come to terms with the human situation, on the other to lay a claim for the rights of the individual. That any of them were created under ideal conditions would have drawn derision from their composers. The "golden age" was always gone.

Collectively the Renaissance and Baroque periods occupy not less than three centuries of history: a long stretch of time. Artistically and intellectually speaking it was a period of phenomenal energy, and within this period it is likely that as much music was composed as in the interval between then and now. It was a formative period in which the foundations of common musical experience were laid. At the beginning of the period art music was confined by functional purpose, and its enjoyment limited to a minority. At the end of the period it was, as near as makes no odds, available for the many. Further, in the first instance the character of music and the forms it adopted were determined by the Church and the secular ruler, the two often working together. In the second, the claims of the first institution to legislate in the general field of aesthetics had lost validity, while the ruler's prerogatives to patronage were beginning gradually to be eroded by economic forces, and by philosophical argument.

The crucial phase in this transition were the years lying between the Lutheran Reformation (which effectively started in 1517) and the death of Elizabeth I of England. During these years from the musician's point of view the madrigal became as important as the Mass or the motet, instrumental music began to shake itself free from the bondage of vocal techniques, and old conceptions of tonality gave place to new. During the sixteenth century European man, emboldened by the liberating influences of new religious experience, of literary and scientific discoveries, and by the anticipation of an enhanced standard of living, shifted his sights from a future hitherto defined in grim terms by theologians, to the present. When one says European man, one means the more fortunate European man – in general the one who was secure within an aristocratic environment. Sixteenth century culture is spattered with the names of princes, dukes, and counts, to many of whom we are indebted for their persistence in the pursuit of humanism. This pursuit was not undertaken without some self-interest. Medieval music, in theory at least, was considered as a tribute to God. Renaissance music, as countless dedications show, was intended as a means of enhancing the sometimes otherwise doubtful reputation of the patron.

When Nicholas Yonge published his epoch-making collection of Italian madrigals – with two by William Byrd included – with English texts, *Musica Transalpina*, in 1588, he dedicated it to Lord Gilbert Talbot. "But seeking yet a stronger string to my bow", he wrote in his "Epistle dedicatorie",

I thought good in all humble and duetifull sort to offer my selfe and my bold attempt to the defence and prótection of your Lordship, to whose honourable hands I present the same. Assuring myselfe, that so great is the love and affection which hee beareth to your L. as the view of your name on the Front of the Bookes, will take away all displeasure and unkindnes from mee ...

An astute man, for he had in mind a broad market of music-lovers to exploit, Nicholas Yonge was thus paying lip-service to the principle of aristocratic superiority but also using a noble name as a selling aid. By 1588 music was being published in quantity, and this was another factor that influenced both its character and the extent of its public.

Three-quarters of the Renaissance music that we are likely to hear is not only fairly narrowly functional, but also evoked by or associated with words. As has been suggested one feature of the change from Renaissance to Baroque was the emancipation of instruments. It is likely that the amateur who is no more than generally aware of the Baroque will base his awareness for the most part on instrumental music, suites, sonatas, and, more especially, a particular kind of concerto described as *concerto grosso*. The stock Baroque names are those of Corelli, Vivaldi, Telemann, Bach, and Handel.

A cursory view of the lists of the compositions of these composers underlines the conclusion that the period was one of enormous activity. The Church – now more accurately the Churches – although less powerful than formerly was still socially effective and continued to offer plenty of scope to the musician. The aristocracy, a cohesive and powerful economic and cultural force, that in the latter connection operated on an international scale, was not yet past the peak of its power; and not one of the composers named above was indifferent to the fact, even though two of them (Telemann and Handel) opted out of the system. Telemann and Handel spent the most of their lives respectively in Hamburg and London, where middle class standards prevailed, and where there was less of autocracy than elsewhere. Both Telemann and Handel tried to capitalise on the rapidly growing middle-class enthusiasm for music. Most of the instrumental music of the former was designed for amateur performance, while the oratorios of the latter were primarily addressed to the London bourgeoisie.

In more or less modern times composers have been in the habit of mitigating present disappointment by an optimistic assumption that they would gain the applause of posterity. Tchaikovsky more than once, observed that "his time would come". Mahler used the same words. The effect of such aspirations has been disastrous. Not least of all so far as the listener is concerned. He is drawn to the conclusion that what is of today can only be "understood" tomorrow. The composer – if he is unfortunate enough to have inherited the psychopathic strain from his Romantic predecessor – is in danger of trying to satisfy the fallacy by a kind of wilful obscurantism. The Renaissance or Baroque composer would have found this attitude distinctly odd, and deplorable. His job was to provide music, and when one commission was executed to get on with the next.

The fertility of composers was staggering. In spite of the fact that many manuscripts disappeared Orlando di Lasso turned out well over 1000 compositions, while Vivaldi wrote at least 500 concertos, and Telemann 1000 overtures alone. Apart from other works of various kinds Handel wrote about 40 operas and 20 or so oratorios, while Bach's church cantatas that are still in existence are around the 200 mark.

Before such abundance of invention one stands helpless. Or one feels that one ought to do so. Yet the industry of the Baroque composers helps to dispel some of our uncertain values. It suggests that we treat a work on its merits without stopping to consider whether or not it qualifies as "great music". Half a dozen works in a decade, perhaps, are indisputably that, and are so accepted. But beyond those works is a vast territory open to inspection. How vast this territory is is indicated by the rough and ready statistics of the last paragraph.

It is fair to say that Baroque composers were energetic, particularly when it is remembered that they were, without exception, also the principal executant musicians of this time.

It is also fair to say that Baroque music is energetic. That this is so stems from the rhythmic impulses on which it was based. The rhythmic pulsation of, say, the first movement of the Third Brandenburg Concerto (although any instrumental movement of the period will do) is the impression first received and last forgotten. In a beat-conscious generation Bachian dynamism has a new fascination, even if helped on by quasi-pop groups. It may very well be that the latter ("Les Swingles" *et al*) have got somewhere near the heart of the matter.

In general terms Baroque has a wider significance, that may be translated as exuberance. This quality is evident not merely in rhythmic terms, but also in the frequent and rich ornamentation that distinguishes the melodic line. The extent to which ornamentation was a vital part of the Baroque system is best realised by listening particularly to the slow movements of the Bach Concertos, or to the Preludes and Fantasias for organ. Bach was precise in this matter. He wrote his ornamentation into his works. Many composers left it to the performer.

It is generally assumed that music is finalised by its composer, and that the written score is the warrant for all further executant action. It should, at this stage, be made clear that this is a quite recent concept. Until the end of the Baroque era a great deal was left to the inventiveness of the performer and extemporisation was a large part of any Baroque performance. This, too, is a mark of exuberance. Because scores of the Baroque period left out certain details – especially of ornamentation – the latest generation of musicologists have been busy putting the matter to rights. Sometimes one is bound to wonder whether non-composers and non-performers are the best hands at restoring the impression of spontaneous creativity that the original performers were intended to convey. *Messiah* has become a regular parade-ground for musicological exercise, as the listener will discover by comparing various contemporary performances.

On the whole Baroque art is spacious, and musical works are of some considerable dimension. Although during the Renaissance era the progress was towards spaciousness the impression gained from listening to music of that period is that it was more concerned with fineness of detail than with broader effects. The norm of Renaissance music was the motet (restricted by the scale of the text), the Mass (in general, a sequence of five sections intended not to be performed as a whole but interspersed in liturgical action), and the madrigal (after the formal pattern of a motet but often owing some allegiance to the spirit of folk song). Attitudes to rhythm in music of this kind were dictated by characteristics of verbal rhythm on the one hand, and the mathematics of note quantities on the other. Part of the fascination of a work for voices of this period is the intricacy of the rhythmic structure, in which the individual rhythms of separate and independent voices interlock. The situation is, of course, clarified if one takes part in the performance of such music. Madrigals, for instance, were rather to be sung than to be listened to. The whole of the music of this period was conceived in terms of a few rather than a large number of performers. The motets, Masses, and madrigals, were often left to a single voice to a part.

We thus begin to adjust our ears to situations. The earlier music of the Western tradition that is to be encountered on record demands a particular kind of involvement. The inner character of the music, to be appreciated to some extent from its context, is more significant than the shape it assumes in terms of sonorities. In the Baroque era the sonorities themselves became a predominant issue. In 1500 the palette of tone-colours was limited. Two hundred years later it was much more extensive. Two hundred years after that the possibilities were endless; so much so that there was a tendency to shut up shop and to return to the purity of earlier times. Hence one cause of the return to some of the values of antiquity.

The home of the Renaissance was Italy, and cultural developments in that country, from the fourteenth to the eighteenth centuries, affected every other European country. From early times every country had its own forms of musical expression, but until the time of the Reformation these were related to the ecclesiastical centre of Europe – Rome – by means of the plainchant melodies that were an integral part of a universal liturgy. Plainchant existed by itself, but it had been woven into the texture of choral music when this emerged as a competent vehicle for musical thought. The choir of the late medieval and Renaissance period was of men alone, or of boys and men. The exclusion of women from participation in sacred choral music was due to the fact that they were ineligible for the priesthood, and the singing-men (often ordained) and boys were regarded as executing at least quasi-priestly functions.

The idea that a choir of boys and men has a particular virtue is still maintained, and the popularity of such choirs as those of King's College, Cambridge, the Vienna Boys' Choir and the Choir of St. Thomas's, Leipzig, rests on this idea. The facts responsible for such conditions of performance have been transmuted into a latter-day mystique. Out of this mystique has emerged the twentieth century counter-tenor, who may very well be a fine artist in his own right but (on the principle that one swallow does not make a summer) does not in himself re-create the age of the Renaissance or the Baroque. There is a danger that the cult of authenticity creates its own illusions, and that the new scientists of music are but disguised romantics.

The most famous musical organisation of the sixteenth century was the choir of the Sistine Chapel. The most notable composer associated with this choir was Palestrina. A figure of considerable influence in his own time, and one who has achieved an even greater posthumous fame, Palestrina summarised many centuries of achievement. He is, to speak in sight-seeing terms, not to be missed.

Palestrina worked with what now might seem limited resources – the medium of unaccompanied voices. His aim was to provide the services and ceremonies of the Church with appropriate music: that is music of a sumptuousness worthy of its setting but not so self-evident that it impeded its main purpose – to educate the worshipper to his duties as a worshipper. That he could indulge either in self-expression or in the expression of common emotional habits was an idea alien to the ecclesiastical composer of that period. He was there, so to speak, to state the facts of the case. The clearest exposition of indifference to annotation is the *Missa Papae Marcelli* composed in answer to a Papal request for a work in which "everything could be both heard and understood properly". On one side of this stands the

45

great motet *Tu es Petrus*, on the other the setting of the ancient Passiontide hymn (or sequence) *Stabat mater dolorosa*.

In all cases Palestrina builds musical textures out of imitatively interdependent parts, contrasted with homophonic slabs of choral note-clusters of varying intensity. The aptness of the motet to a Papal ceremony and of the hymn to the theme of the Crucifixion was evident to the worshipper on account of the other apparatus of worship. To us it is only evident either by stretching the imagination to take in the external imagery or by considering the content of the texts, and by discovering some relevance to our own circumstances in either or both. Otherwise it is likely that we consider this music as having an absolute quality.

I suspect that music which has this apparently absolute, passionless, quality exerts an equally beneficial influence as that which is more impassioned. According to classical theories concerning the arts the latter type is that which "purges the emotions". I doubt whether this is the case in music, for one very good reason. The emotional content of a work in the end is entirely a subjective matter for the listener. And this is in spite of palpable efforts to broaden the vocabulary of music so as to make it a competent vehicle for the expression of particularised emotion.

Now the music which is summarised by that of Palestrina – the general style being found all over Europe – is pellucid in statement. Melodic lines are consistent with what readily lies within the singer's range, while the interweaving lines of related melodic motivs are firmly bound within a simple harmonic framework, of which the main supports are diatonic (i.e. nonchromatic), so-called common, chords. Of these some are major and some are minor. The whole belongs, in theory, at least, to the system of modes that had been systematised from the ancient plainsong melodies.

The modal system (to be recognised from listening to plainsong) like any system was varied, sometimes impulsively and spontaneously by singers, sometimes deliberately by composers. It was particularly susceptible to variation under the influence of harmonic expansion. Towards the end of the sixteenth century lip-service was paid to modal organisation by theorists but in practice something approaching the familiar major-minor scale structure was in sight. Moreover there was an increasing tendency to mark off sections of works by formalised endings on new tonics (thus giving the appearance of a new tonal centre being used) and to add chromatic chords to the basic diatonic note groups. Both tendencies increased the colour potential of music and in so doing also increased the means whereby emotions could at least be symbolised.

We speak of the Renaissance and the Baroque periods as though they were separate entities. In truth the two were so intermingled that it is not really possible to separate the one from the other. If emotional expression is a yard-stick then it is difficult to avoid the striking quality of the music of Orlando di Lasso – a Fleming, who worked in Italy, and in 1556 began his long career as director of music at the Court of the Duke of Bavaria, in Munich. Lasso was a man of feeling. This is evident from his letters – the first by a musician to survive and to give an idea of personality. It is also evident from the range of his works as well as their character. He composed madrigals – the typical Italianate part-song that was the secular counterpart to the motet – but also made less courtly arrangements of German and French folk-songs. He composed masses, motets, and *Penitential Psalms*. The range, then, is from a broad humour, through an elegance derived from Italian models, to what later was to be defined as a typically German kind of expression. This was often dark in colour, disquieting by reason of the placing of discord, and centred on the theme of death. Orlando di Lasso was among the early composers of Passion music. His influence lasted right down until the time of Bach.

Palestrina composed madrigals, but Italian masters who were more versatile in this field were Luca Marenzio and Giovanni Croce. These, and many other, composers fed the growing demand for secular music in the home. The fashion of madrigal singing spread rapidly, in many cases overtaking existing traditions of dramatic part-singing. The madrigal, both in respect of words and music, was stylised, and, as in the case of the style of church music, was universally adopted.

In Britain a craze for madrigal singing was triggered off by the publication of Yonge's *Musica Transalpina*. Thereafter a whole company of English composers set to and turned out madrigals for the benefit of Italophile gentlemen lately returned from a transalpine holiday full of musical enthusiasm, and for the benefit of those who thought it the right thing to do to imitate their superiors. In England the madrigals of Morley, Wilbye, Weelkes, Byrd, Gibbons, Bennet, and many others, were not only masterpieces of musical ingenuity, but also often delightfully descriptive of country life and custom. German madrigals, too, had their own individuality, and were frequently of an earthy and sometimes even satirical character. In both England and Germany, where new traditions of church music had grown up round the vernacular and, in the second case, around the chorale, the social criticism that arose from the maelstrom of the Reformation infected the character of the music. To such an extent that one may now begin to speak of national music.

Madrigals, as well as church music (except in the Sistine Chapel) were more often than not accompanied by instruments. As secular standards began to prevail over ecclesiastical ones instrumental music began tentatively to lead an independent existence. The anthems, motets, madrigals, were transferred to consorts of wind or string instruments (viols), which also were suited with arrangements of dance tunes. The general repertoire was also adopted for keyboard instruments – for the organ, for the virginals, for the harpsichord. On the eve of the seventeenth century independent instrumental works (which none the less advertised their debt to vocal styles) existed in the shape of *ricercari*, *fantasias* (both contrapuntal in nature) toccatas and variations (which exploited the possibilities of the keyboard), as well as in sets of dances. The instrumental piece designed after the madrigalian manner, but adapted to instrumental behaviour, was in England termed the *Fancy* (= Fantasia). This form persisted right down to the time of Purcell, in whom Renaissance and Baroque met, whose Fantasias (3–7 parts) are among the most striking testimonials to the genius of a composer who treated what was old and what was new on merit.

The late Renaissance (or early Baroque) composer was in an enviable condition compared with his predecessors. He had a hitherto unparalleled range of sonorities, instrumental and vocal, at his disposal. None exploited these sonorities more effectively than Giovanni Gabrieli, in whose *Sacrae Symphoniae* (and here the term *symphony* makes its appearance) solo voices, contrasting choruses set in facing galleries, and instruments were all combined in cohesive works of which the structure was determined largely by the disposition of various effects of sonority. Gabrieli was employed at St. Mark's Cathedral, Venice, which then became a place of pilgrimage for foreign visitors and composers. Among the latter the principal was Heinrich Schütz, who brilliantly married Venetian ideals of sonorousness with Saxon traditions of choral music. The German motet (voices and instruments) often incorporating chorale melodies, was the mainstay of the Lutheran church, and, practised by many hands, it grew at a later stage into the church cantata.

The additional colour thus imparted to music, enhanced by the chromatic experiments of later Italian madrigalists such as Carlo Gesualdo, signified a search for dramatic values. Music with a theatrical purpose had been long practised – in Court entertainments, in civic and royal pageants, and in the sacred plays that in central Europe culminated in the Passion play (which in turn gave way to the purely musical Passion).

The generally humanistic tendencies of the sixteenth century, illustrated in all the arts and especially in literature, led to a revitalisation of drama. Inevitably the relationship of music to drama (always close) came under review. Polyphonic music had its palpable disadvantages from the dramatic point of view. To make love, or to die (which activities are what all drama is about), in five- or six-part counterpoint, and to do so convincingly, was not easy. So, for theatrical purposes, counterpoint was out.

The seventeenth century got under way with *recitative*, to which was soon attached *aria*, and out of the conjunction of the two came the concept of opera, by the side of which stood the recitative-aria sequence known as cantata which was cultivated more privately than opera. Opera, passing through the hands of Monteverdi and Alessandro Scarlatti, became the most exciting and colourful entertainment of the seventeenth century. Conjoi tly, since the Catholic Church was now alive to the virtues inherent in the dramatic style of music, there developed a form of sacred opera, classified, in view of its emergence within the walls of a Roman oratory, as oratorio.

Music is, of course, a form of ostentation. In simple terms the performing musician is by nature an exhibitionist. In the early Baroque period exhibitionism led to the conscious cult of virtuosity. Brilliance of execution was expected, and performers were quick to oblige. Singers, since opera was the high point of music, were at the head of the profession, but were closely followed by violinists – the violin now having replaced the less sonorous viol. Singers and violinists showed an interest in a top-line melody, now accompanied by the chordal background provided by an obliging harpsichordist who made up the accompaniment as best he could from the *figured bass* that was all he had to play from.

The history of music is the record of a series of shifts of emphasis, of variations of balance between relationships. In pre-Baroque music it was the music itself that was important, performers and composers were taken for granted. In early Baroque the position of the composer vis-à-vis his audience (i.e. the patron, and his acquaintances) was stronger, and the inventive capacity of the composer became more patent. In middle Baroque, music now being a more public art, the place of the performer (or of the composer as a performer) was much more considerable. That is to say, his earning power was considerably increased, and with it his independence. The growth of opera, and the erection of opera-houses, was significant in two ways. First, it drew attention to the pictorial and emotional properties inherent in music. Second, by virtue of its structure, it made an effective division between performer and audience. The kind of music that belonged to opera was not, as had previously been the case, music in which participation by the amateur was not only possible but desirable but music belonging to a spectacle. Music, therefore, became more spectacular.

The modern music-lover looks back to what he considers "old music" from premises which were established during the eighteenth century. The public presentation of music in the twentieth century is undeniably spectacular; to the extent that the audience quite consciously goes to the concert hall to see as well as to hear. Now since techniques improve standards of virtuosity alter; what once was difficult of accomplishment is, in a technical sense, not so any more.

Once upon a time it was only Couperin who could properly play the Ordres (Suites) of Couperin. In his day Bach was the wonder of Germany not on account of the musical quality of his organ works, but because he was the only organist capable of performing them. Now neither Couperin nor Bach present serious technical problems to the really efficient graduate from a school of music. This being the case modern attitudes to works of the Baroque era have centred on (a) the correct reading of the scores – especially in respect of note-lengths and ornaments, (b) the possibility of re-introducing improvisation, and (c) the choice and balance of instrumental sonorities. The guiding spirit behind the modern performance of both Renaissance and Baroque music is the editor.

Let us return to the working conditions of Baroque music. First, the composer was content to consider the present and not the future. Taking into account the terms of his commission he composed pieces as and when required. If by chance a repetition of a work was requested he regarded the second performance as a new creative venture – to the extent that he could vary it as he wished. The discrepancies between various manuscripts of the oratorios and operas of Handel, for instance, make it quite impossible ever to arrive at that pride of the editorial heart – a "definitive edition". But within the context of performance in church, salon, opera-house, or public music-room the composer was aware that his status was appreciating. Formally a craftsman, he was now invested with the standing of a public orator.

The personality of the composer becomes apparent when he dominates a situation. In musical terms this means the provision of large works. Hence the arrival in Baroque times of the *Suite* and the *Concerto grosso*.

51

Suites proliferated from the time of Purcell to that of Bach and Handel, many being composed for the harpsichord, but there being no difference of pattern between a keyboard suite and an orchestral suite. The essence of the suite was the aggregation of separate pieces of different character. The contrasts implied by the preludes, allemandes, courantes, gigues, and so on (all but the first signifying dances) of the Partitas of Bach were considerable; but controlled by the unity imposed by a common key centre. Largeness, in fact, only exists where there is unity. And it was a searching for unified structures that exercised the minds of composers when music became a public art.

The *concerto grosso* was based on the stabilisation of the instrumental ensemble of string orchestra, supported by harpsichord, with or without recorders (flutes), oboes, bassoons, trumpets, or anything else that might be available. The two pioneer masters of concerto grosso were Corelli, a Roman, and Vivaldi, a Venetian. Their conception of concerto grosso was a synthesis. The old contrasting effects of alternating groups of sonorities was adopted, so that what was played by an expert leading group of players (the *concertino*) was taken up, or backed, by the main body (hence the term *concerto grosso*). The first movement of a concerto grosso, and this runs throughout the period, is a sequence of statements of a principal motiv (the ritornello), contrasted with texturally varied interludes, moved through a circle of related tonalities, and held together by a firm, consistent, rhythm. The importance of rhythmic stability was great; if only because Baroque music was played without the active presence of a conductor. (The first violinist led, and the harpsichordist also had some responsibility for maintaining control). In the concerto the concertino element was variable. It could consist of the principals of the string section – without the viola, which was as yet an unfavoured instrument – or of wind instruments, or a mixture of both, or of a solo instrument.

Succeeding concerto grosso movements borrowed from the aria, dance, and fugal patterns otherwise established. Hence we note the synthesis that was the Baroque concerto, with form but not unduly formalised. The process of tidying up the loose ends came at a later stage.

A minimal collection of Baroque instrumental music would include sonatas (or concertos) by Corelli, Vivaldi, Handel, and Bach, the four inter-acting composers who commanded the last years of the seventeenth and the first half of the eighteenth centuries. Since a natural inclination leads to the larger rather than the smaller (tonally speaking), and to the known (by reputation that is) rather than to the unknown, it is probable that the collector will land up with the so-called "Christmas" Concerto of Corelli – so named because the last movement is based on a favourite Italian Nativity motiv of the period, the "Four Seasons" of Vivaldi, the Brandenburg Concertos of Bach, and the "Water" and "Fireworks" Music of Handel.

As it happens this selection crosses neatly from the private to the public, from the aristocratic towards the democratic, and in so doing indicates a momentous shift in musical function.

Corelli wrote for a select audience, assembled in a Roman Cardinal's drawing-room. Handel's "Fireworks" Music, to celebrate the Peace of Aix-la-Chapelle, was performed for a general audience in a London Pleasure Garden in 1749. Certain features are to be found in Corelli and Handel (who, as a young man, knew Corelli in Rome), as also in Vivaldi and Bach. First, in the main movements, the ritornello principle: that is the design of a large-scale movement around a recurring section. Second, the addition of dance movements to the main ritornello designed movement. Third, the extension of the antiphonal principle to the instrumental ensemble. Corelli's concerto contrasted the small group of section leaders (1st and 2nd violin, and cello) with the main body.

The Baroque principle of *concerto grosso* and *concertino* is one starting-point for latter-day instrumentation, and, in terms of Romantic music, we have the *Introduction and Allegro* of Elgar, and the *Fantasia on a theme of Thomas Tallis* by Vaughan Williams, both for string quartet and string orchestra, and both masterly in their appreciation of the tonal values inherent in the medium.

Corelli was the first great master of the string orchestra. Vivaldi, a musician of the Venetian school, was a brilliant investigator of sonorities, and in place of the concertino that

Corelli regularised often substituted a single instrument. The "Four Seasons" cycle of concerti, fancifully borrowing their title from poetry, are in fact violin concertos. Vivaldi himself was a violinist, and as music teacher in a girls' school (an orphanage famous for its music) a number of his concertos were probably composed for teaching purposes. Bach was a keen student of Vivaldi, and made arrangements of a large number of Vivaldi's concertos. His own works in this form, composed for varying instrumental resources, were, not surprisingly, influenced by Vivaldi, and in general in line with Vivaldi's three movement patterns. The vigour of the D minor Concerto for two violins is a fine tribute to the stimulation afforded by the Vivaldian concerto. This work is otherwise interesting on account of its existence in another form, in C minor and for two harpsichords. Thus we see how the contrast between *concertino* and *concerto grosso* was more important to the composer than particular tone colours within the concertino.

The Brandenburg Concertos, composed when Bach was director of music at the Court of Anhalt-Cöthen, are the complete summary of the Baroque intention in so far as orchestral music was concerned. Dedicated to the Margrave of Brandenburg (in the hope of establishing himself in princely circles) Bach went out of his way to expose his talents. Thus these concertos show a marvellous variety of invention, and of sonorities. The sonorities, however, were exploited because they were there to exploit, and not because of a predetermination to use them for their own sake. The first is for the obsolete violino piccolo (a small violin tuned in fifths from middle C), 3 oboes, 2 horns, bassoon, strings, and, of course, harpsichord; the second, for violin, flute, oboe, trumpet soloists; the fourth, for violin and two flutes; the fifth, for violin, flute, and harpsichord. The third and sixth are for strings alone.

Surrounded as he was by competent colleagues and accustomed to music-club conditions (even more when he moved to Leipzig) Bach was very much free to follow his own devices in these works. Hence their range of interest and their complexity.

With Handel, a much more public figure, it was otherwise.

Music by Handel – probably part of the "Water Music" – was played on the Thames on July 17, 1717. (In fact the pieces now collected as "The Water Music" comprises two separate sets, the one in F major, the other in D major, of which the former are most generally known.) On this occasion a royal party went in barges from Whitehall to Chelsea, and back again, during which one bargeload of "50 instruments of all sorts . . . played all the way from Lambeth the finest symphonies, compos'd express for this occasion by Mr. Handel."

Open-air music was no new phenomenon, and "Water-music" was written before Handel immortalised the term. What Handel did, both in this and the later Firework Music, was to broaden the whole concept of orchestral music, to attune it to the general ear, first by an infectious tunefulness (exemplified by the famous "Air" of the *Water Music*) and then by a direct appeal to the appreciation of the audience by means of bold orchestral colouring – bolder colouring than the fashion of the salon admitted.

In the widest sense Handel was a popular composer, his works known to the great mass of the people of London. Baroque art set out to capture the attention of the many rather than the few. Its final triumph in this respect was in the works of Handel which, in one sense before their time in their social appeal, outlasted it. The "popular" works of Handel swept round the classical era and directly into the province of the modern concept of mass media. How this happened is described in Chapter 9.

4

Classical Music

TERMINOLOGY lays many traps before the incautious, for
there is always a sizeable gap between what a word means and
what it is generally thought to mean. No words have caused
more frustration than those which figure most prominent in the
vocabulary of the arts – "classical", "romantic", "modern",
and "popular". At this juncture our concern is primarily with
the first. In the context in which it has been made to appear it is
seen at once to be on the defensive; for in popular understanding "romantic", "modern" and "popular", are appreciated as
its natural enemies. Yet, for "classical" there is a kind of general,
if grudging, admiration. There may be heard, "I don't understand classical music"; behind which lies the unspoken wish
to be able to understand, and so to graduate to the company of
the elect.

In the wider sense "classical" stands directly opposite to
"popular". Thus all music that is excluded from classification
under the latter heading tends to be lumped together as classical
– whether composed by Bach or Britten, Purcell or Prokofiev,
Schubert or Schoenberg. The objection to this definition
lies less in the definition itself than in the overtones that it
carries.

Among these overtones one detects the supposition that
classical music, in this sense, is weighted with a load of re-
spectability. Up to a point this idea has rubbed off from the
apparent quality and status, in a social and historic connotation,
of those who have supported classical music by their patronage.
Thus there is a danger of finding oneself bogged down by
notions of social division that have nothing immediately to do

with the matter, even though there is a certain psychological backlog to be cleared.

Passing from social to moral consideration we next find "classical" as being synonymous with "good". The worst teachers are those who drop the word "uplifting" into a discussion. In the broad category of classical music there is good music and there is bad music. The bad music is bad because it is dull. As for music that is accepted as being good the criterion is an aesthetic one; goodness in this sense is overtly neither on the side of morality or amorality. The "Jupiter" Symphony of Mozart, which may fairly be described as an example of good, classical, music, may have somewhat increased the sum total of human happiness; but it has not, so far as I know, led directly to any diminution in either lustful or criminal tendencies.

It may be argued, but not very convincingly, that the *St. Matthew Passion* and *Messiah*, have been potent in effecting moral improvement. If so, then so at a particular period Gounod's *Redemption* and Stainer's *Crucifixion* were also effective agents in this respect; though it would be difficult to maintain, if this were the case, that the quality of the music had anything to do with it. The factor that matters in this connection is the words. The further away it is from words the more musical music is. A complete absence of a verbal element leaves music, to a greater or lesser degree, in an abstract condition. This brings us to another sanctified term – "absolute music"; music that is neither more nor less than music, that is self-contained, that is to be appreciated, analysed, and understood only within the framework of musical values.

The ideal of absolute music is attractive, but unattainable. On the one hand the whole apparatus of musical design is so involved with in-built points of reference that cannot be forgotten by the listener that it is subject to observations that are at least affected by extra-musical values. On the other hand, a musical work is defined inevitably by the personality of its author. In both cases emotional factors supervene. And it is these that provide the great impediment to the viability of any convincing theory of absoluteness.

The notion of absoluteness, however, is somewhat maintained

by nomenclature. In general the instrumental works of Mozart, Haydn, and Beethoven, are not known by titles but by numbers. (There are exceptions, but these can wait.) Beethoven's Fifth Symphony – so far as externals are concerned – is neither more nor less than a fifth symphony, and it has never been suggested that this work would benefit if it were otherwise designated. Nor would any such designation make any difference to the enjoyment of the listener. At the same time Beethoven himself observed that behind this work lay the idea of "Destiny knocking at the door".

The facts of this Symphony are: that it consists of four separate movements; that the relationship of one to another is marked by melodic, rhythmic, and harmonic statements comprising sequences of theses and antitheses, of apparent questions and answers, all of which are held together by the fact that the music operates within a defined zone. This zone is recognisable by the limitations within which the composer works. The instrumental forces are greater than those employed by Vivaldi and less than those used by Richard Strauss. Otherwise the obvious limiting factor is the structure of tonality. Beethoven here works within the margins of C minor-major tonality, with all digressions therefrom qualified by an underlying theory of compatibility. The prevailing tonal climate implies a disposition towards a particular kind of musical character, and this character springs from attitudes to tonal values held at a particular period – the Classical Period.

The Classical Period, in music, includes Haydn, Mozart, and Beethoven, three composers especially associated with Vienna during the period of that city's pre-eminence in musical affairs, who constituted the structures of sonata-style and established the final independence of instrumental music in various forms. These composers in fact created a new attitude to music. By so doing they established an image that has remained a guiding principle, which is accepted in broad terms as the classical tradition. By reference to this tradition it becomes possible to include within it composers who did not belong to the Classical Period. The notable influence is that of Brahms, whose symphonies, concertos, and chamber music, are seen to be classical by intention.

The symphony (to take the most obvious form of the classical) is by way of being comprehensive – inclusive rather than exclusive. The symphony is the meeting-point of song and of dance, of the lyrical and the dramatic, though all three elements are, ideally, sublimated. This comprehensiveness is also a sign of absoluteness, in that it indicates the many-sidedness of music within itself. Inevitably, the composition of a symphonic work entails rejection and selection, and the arrangement of whatever is selected within a meaningful framework. A symphony, since it is schematically disposed, requires logical preparation; in the end it may appear to have followed a logical course. We speak of the "logic" of a symphony without, perhaps, more conviction than is given by a personal evaluation, or by acceptance of another opinion. But the root of the matter does, in fact, lie in the word logic. The pursuit of logic, of reason rather than unreason, led to the circumstances that made the development of classical music both desirable and possible. The period in which the symphony came into effective existence is that in which the cult of reason reached its apogee before it was overtaken by the cult of unreason. The hidden hand behind the phase of music defined as classical is a French hand. At the beginning there was Voltaire, at the end Rousseau.

The Renaissance impulse was Italian. The Renaissance passed into the age of the Enlightenment. The precision of thought that distinguished the apostles of the Enlightenment led to a regard for social orderliness, to a refinement of behaviour, and to a nice formality in expression. The influence of the Enlightenment was strong in Germany, and throughout the eighteenth century the tendency was towards a reduction of the indigenous elements within German music to accommodate a higher degree of elegance. Even while J. S. Bach was still active in Leipzig a new fashion was establishing itself in that city. The songs of "Sperontes" (the name by which J. S. Schulze was known), based on minuets, polonaises, marches, and so on, were immensely popular; so much so that they were purchased by Leopold Mozart, far off in Salzburg, and given to his son Wolfgang. The influence of "Sperontes" is evident in the operetta *Bastien and Bastienne* – in its artificiality and prettiness a characteristic offspring of the North German idea of Enlightenment.

From his earliest years the internationally minded Telemann had been a devoted student of French music, and the clarity that he admired therein, is reflected in almost every instrumental work that he composed. At Mannheim, on the Rhine, the Elector Karl Theodor was so Francophile that in 1773 it could be observed that the town was more like a French colony than a German town. A keen musician, playing the flute and the cello, Karl Theodor was determined that the culture of his Court should be of distinguished character. That music took pride of place in general esteem was due not so much to the Elector's personal inclinations but to the fact that he employed a team of outstanding talents. Among them were Johann Stamitz, of an immigrant family of Bohemian musicians, Carlo Giuseppe Toeschi, an Italian, and Ignaz Holzbauer, a peripatetic Austrian. Working with the Italian opera overture as model, these were among the first to compose works of symphonic pattern and significance that, as a contemporary writer put it, "first surpassed the bounds of common opera overtures." For a long time such works were indifferently titled overtures or symphonies. Lucid in design pieces of this order obeyed the conditions of *galanterie* necessitated by deference to French ideals of clarity.

But music only takes on meaning in performance. The Mannheim orchestra was acknowledged to be one of the finest in Europe. Apart from the unanimity with which it played it was notable for its range of expression. Its *forte* was as thunder, its *crescendo* as a cataract, its *diminuendo* the splashing of a distant brook, its *piano* was a rustle of spring: so it was said by Christian Schubart.

We have, in later times, become so accustomed to considering human activities in terms of nationality (even though the fallacies of this are painfully evident) that we miss one essential point of the classical spirit in music. This sprang if not from an indifference to nationality, at least from a desire to co-ordinate the best endeavours of all traditions and conventions. The Mannheim School was multi-national. Mozart, son of a

German, native of a "free city" (politically neither German nor Austrian), was for practical purposes an Austrian, but at home in any part of Europe. Haydn owed allegiance to Austria also, but his origins were very mixed. Classical music began by being super-national.

The "expression" represented by familiar dynamic terms was built into the nature of early symphony. Nor were Christian Schubart's analogies quite fortuitous. Their imagery was taken from the lavish entertainments (half theatrical, half musical) that were among the chief attractions of the summer season when the Mannheim Court transferred to the summer residence at Schwetzingen. Behind the Mannheim Symphony there was, implicit at least, a programme.

Meanwhile other attempts to accommodate the spirit of the age were being made elsewhere. In Berlin, and, later, in Hamburg, Carl Philipp Emanuel Bach was rationalising the old style concerto and sonata within a *galant* idiom. A prolific composer, whose reputation during his lifetime was far greater than that his father had enjoyed, C. P. E. Bach explored almost every possibility. From the Italian sonata he adapted the customary two-theme first movement structure, but enlarged it. He introduced recitative-like patterns into slow movements. He adopted idioms from operatic aria and from middle German keyboard practice. Although C. P. E. Bach is considered (if at all) because he evolved the first movement pattern later described as "sonata form" his music was relished because of its frequent unexpectedness, its changes of key, figuration, and tonality. In short, Bach produced music that satisfied both the taste for virtuoso performance and the wish that music should be more rather than less expressive. Living at the same time as Goethe and Schiller, C. P. E. Bach also absorbed and recreated something of the *Sturm und Drang* tendencies in the literature of his time.

It thus becomes clear that the music of the period was intended to be comprehensive, both in structure and emotional content. One significant feature was the gradual replacement of the harpsichord by the pianoforte – the popularity of which was ensured by its more comprehensive nature. The establishment of the pianoforte in public esteem led to a greater interest in keyboard virtuosity and to the emergence of the classical piano concerto, of which not only C. P. E. Bach, but also his brothers Wilhelm Friedemann and Johann Christian were pioneers.

C. P. E. Bach was thirty-six years old when his father died, and well established in his career. When he died Ludwig van Beethoven was already eighteen years of age, and had lately visited Vienna where he had been praised by Mozart. These facts somewhat impinge on any ideas of an extensive and exclusive "Classical Period" and show how in fact the development (as it is called) of music is at least an uncertain, leap-frogging, process.

A feature of European musical life in the eighteenth century was the establishment of the concert. Musical performances at Court, and in the houses of the wealthy, had a long history. But the organisation of regular series of concerts by societies was relatively new. Such series took place under the aegis of culti-vated aristocrats, of Universities, and of the middle classes. There were famous concerts in Berlin, Frankfurt, Leipzig, Hamburg, Paris, London and Vienna. What with the general mobility of the musical profession, and the fact that orchestral music was published in abundance, a composer could envisage a much wider audience than formerly; and, because of the general availability of music, the tendency towards a universal and international set of values was enhanced. Between the music of Handel, J. S. Bach, and Telemann, there were disparities. A generation later such disparity has all but disappeared, at any rate in respect of style. That this was so is due as much to the freer circulation of music as to a new sense of obedience to a particular concept of musical form.

The classical composers arrived at classical standards at least partly by accident. That classical symphony (and concerto) became firmly associated with Vienna was also more or less fortuitous. As may be concluded from the foregoing any one of three or four celebrated centres of music could have perfected symphonic development.

During the formative period of the symphony the Court of Vienna was served by a number of able musicians. Among these were Georg Christoph, Anton Wagenseil, Georg Reutter, Georg Matthias Monn, and Josef Starzer, all expert in the handling of the overture-symphony style. Between Vienna and Mannheim there were many contacts, since the Mannheim staff included many players and composers who had transferred from Vienna. Wagenseil was a celebrated figure in Vienna when the six-year old Mozart turned up at the Court one day in 1762, "I am," said the precocious boy, "going to play a concerto of yours, and you shall turn over for me." George Reutter was one of Haydn's teachers. The eager amateur inclined to chase up the major masterpieces may at this juncture be gently advised sometimes to relax with the (somewhat rudely assessed) "minor works" by "the lesser masters", without which the major works would never have been possible. The point is made so that the name-dropping that occurs in such a work as this shall not be assumed to be without purpose.

The symphonies of Wagenseil and his Viennese contemporaries were sometimes in three, sometimes in four movements. Haydn's first symphony, composed in 1759, was in three movements. In the next decade, now attached to the Court of Prince Nicholas Esterházy, at Eisenstadt, Haydn wrote about 40 symphonies – of varying pattern and incorporating elements from Italian opera and north German counterpoint. Within this period Mozart composed at least half a dozen symphonies, on which the influence of Johann Christian Bach – the youngest of the Bach sons – was strong. J. C. Bach, who had absorbed the Italian style while cathedral organist in Milan, was not only a master of the epigrammatic phrase but also of discussion of and development of such phrases within the context of sonata procedure (which he had learned in the first place from his brother Carl Philipp Emanuel). Bach was a graceful composer, and by his elegant handling of orchestral sonorities won the esteem of the concert public in London, where he spent the last twenty years of his life.

The *Sturm und Drang* movement (see p. 61) began to take effect when Haydn was in mid-symphonic flight, and when Mozart was approaching what for him was maturity. Haydn's "Farewell" Symphony (no. 45) is hardly *Sturm und Drang*, but, despite its flippant end gesture (the instrumentalists departing one by one in order to advise their employer of their wish to return home from the summer residence in Esterház), it has more than a touch of earnestness. The key signature of F sharp minor was uncommon, while siting the minuet in the key of F sharp major (with six sharps) was at least asking the orchestra for a more than casual consideration of their parts.

The emotional factors which the term *Sturm und Drang* implies are more clearly illustrated by the contrast between Mozart's early G minor symphony (K.183), with its Minuet of serious mien, and that in A major (K.201). The former, composed in 1773, is restless, even morose. The restlessness, which returns within the same tonality in the G minor symphony of 1788 (K.550) is shown not only in the first but also in the last movement. Thus the symphony, of which heretofore the first movement had been regarded as the principal, began to assume an overall character, with some kind of relationship between the movements. In the A major symphony of 1774, a sunny, Austrian work, not far removed from landscape painting, each movement, except the minuet, is in the form of sonata.

This is a point of some significance, for it implies the suzerainty of formal balance, and this has to do with the central principle of eighteenth century philosophy. It also implies a sense of refinement – of ideas if not of manners. Although the manners of the eighteenth century aristocracy were covered with a veneer of elegance they were, on the whole, deplorable. Haydn was well aware of this, but accepted the situation. Mozart, whose temperament lacked the more stable qualities that distinguished Haydn, did not. Nonetheless, both composers accepted the general notion that perfectability of musical form was not only an end to be pursued but that it was within sight. Musical aestheticians of the period were quite firm on this; that the music of the age was the best music that had ever been composed.

"We have," wrote Charles Henri de Blainville, "a kind of music that pleases, is seductive, and paints Nature in new forms . . . The obedient instruments give new beauty to melody and to harmony. Nothing resists them, and everything is

YEHUDI MENUHIN - unique in the affection of music-lovers everywhere through his musicianship and warm humanity.

OTTO KLEMPERER - upholder of the great European conducting tradition and particularly noted for his interpretations of Beethoven and Mahler.

ELISABETH SCHWARZKOPF - the widely admired soprano, equally famous in opera, operetta and lieder.

DIETRICH FISCHER DIESKAU - the supreme interpreter of lieder.
GERALD MOORE - the supreme accompanist.

DANIEL BARENBOIM - pianist and conductor with a phenomenal maturity and musical experience beyond his years.

JACQUELINE DU PRÉ - brilliant young cellist, already established as one of the leading artists of her generation.

JANET BAKER - an artist who combines beauty of voice, warmth of personality and outstanding musicianship.

SIR JOHN BARBIROLLI - Britain's internationally renowned conductor.

VICTORIA DE LOS ANGELES - the enchanting Spanish soprano whose repertoire spans from Purcell to Falla.

SIR ADRIAN BOULT - doyen of British conductors to whom leading British composers have entrusted their first performances.

CARLO MARIA GIULINI - the leading Italian conductor of today.

GERVASE DE PEYER - clarinet virtuoso of the highest distinction and key member of the Melos Ensemble.

MARIA CALLAS - the incomparable prima donna of our time.

NICOLAI GEDDA - the world's most versatile tenor and a musician of rare sensitivity.

JOHN OGDON - dynamic British pianist in the grand tradition.

RAFAEL FRÜHBECK DE BURGOS - the brilliant young Spanish conductor.

delicate and exquisite; there is – in the music – a full explanation, to which we must listen."

This writer was inspired by the programmes of the concerts known collectively as the "Concert Spirituel" in Paris, but the sentiment he expressed was a general one. In considering the internal character of the sonata, the concerto, and the symphony, composers of the second half of the eighteenth century were looking towards a realisation of a common aim: the creation of monuments to the spirit of reason. The best of monuments was to be realised in terms of music since an abstract virtue was most effectively exposed in abstract terms. When, therefore, the four movement symphony assimilated the balanced sonata structure into three principal movements (the dance movement staying as a recollection of the simplicities of life) it seemed that a terminus had been reached.

Form, however, is only the beginning and not the end of music. Haydn and Mozart regularised formal procedures by giving definition to the ideas of their contemporaries. Their significance, however, lies not in their formal procedures, but in what they did with them. Always remembering that the pursuit of reason and formal definition did not exclude the incorporation of emotional properties, indeed, the balance between emotions and the expression of them was the main concern of a classical composer. And the manner of expression depended on the relationship between composer and listener.

The first symphonies and concertos were for intimate occasions. In the period from approximately 1760 to 1790 the symphony orchestra became a powerful, even an overpowering, vehicle of expression. Haydn and Mozart composed in the first place for Austrian audiences. In due course, and with an access of reputation, they composed for the European market. The happy accident of European classical music was, of course, the relationship between Haydn and Mozart, who formed a partnership from which both benefited although neither surrendered any degree of individuality.

In 1787 Mozart's D major Symphony (K.504) was performed in Prague, where Mozart had gone for the production of *The Marriage of Figaro* and where another opera – *Don Giovanni* –

was commissioned. The striking feature of the symphony is the slow introduction to the first movement, which is a foreshadowing of the "Stone Guest" music of *Don Giovanni*. The use of a preludial passage before the statutory first movement is due to Haydn's innovatory zeal, and it gives to the symphonic form a new sense of significance. Apart from the inherent emotional content of an introductory *adagio*, the fact that the easy conventions of the old symphony-overture are thus questioned removes the form from its former theatrical context and establishes its independent dignity. In the Prague Symphony Mozart states the first paragraph in terms of tragedy, with a cold blast of minor tonality prefacing the intention of the symphony proper to function within the festival key of D major. At the same time, and this is characteristic of Mozart, the polarity of major and minor is not lost sight of, for there are consequent references back to the latter tonality.

The classical symphony, as has been stated, had a synoptic quality, and the Mozartian genius for thematic combination is shown in the artless counterpoint of the middle section of the first movement and also of the slow movement – one which also holds the quintessence of Mozartian melody. Here the virtues of song are idealised in instrumental garb, by which it is seen to what extent instrumental sonorities had gained in status.

With both Haydn and Mozart one becomes aware that music if it had become more abstract in one way had become less abstract in another. That is to say, it appears now that music was not first conceived in line and mass to which colour was later applied, but that melody, harmony, and counterpoint were considered from the outset in terms of actual sonority. Which is another way of saying that the orchestra had become important in its own right. This importance was enhanced by the gradual disappearance of an accompanying keyboard instrument. In 1760 the harpsichord (or the piano where it was used) was a vital part of the total scheme. By the 1790s although the piano from which the composer (or his delegate) directed the performance, might be present it was no longer a subscribing member of the tonal ensemble. As a complex of varied sonorities however, the piano had its part to play in opposition to and conjunction with the orchestra in the fully-fledged Mozart piano concerto. In some ways the most personal of Mozart's works (since they sprang from his own ideas of execution and interpretation) his 27 piano concertos cover the widest range of musical and spiritual experience. At one extreme of the emotional spectrum stands the purely lyrical A major Concerto (K.488), significantly with clarinets in the score, at the other the deeply impassioned C minor Concerto (K.491), its urgency underlined by trumpets and drums.

1788 is a memorable date in the history of classical music, for in the summer of that year Mozart composed his three greatest symphonies. The symphonies in E flat (K.543), G minor (K.550), and C major (K.551), are indeed the consummation of the classical ideal in musical composition. The first is a master-piece of lyrical sensibility; the second, of argument within the province of tragedy, the third, of logic. "Mozart's musical expression," said Wagner, "derived its very soul from the delicate vibrations, swellings and accents of the noble style of Italian singing, and was the first to reproduce the effects of this vocal style by means of orchestral instruments." That is what the E flat symphony is about, and in this work one is made aware of the special importance to Mozart of the tone and character of the clarinet. How important this instrument is otherwise testified by the Clarinet Concerto and the Clarinet Quintet, from the tonal point of view two works of a particularly voluptuous quality.

Apart from the famous opening (there is no introduction here) of the G minor symphony the measure of the severity of its cast of thought is apparent in the stern lines of the Minuet, now no longer a light-weight interpretation – after the manner of the *intermezzo* in the *opera seria* – but a means of extending the general argument.

Medieval music had its own mythology (or theology). So it was that modes and rhythmical mensurations had an established order. Because of its symbolic convenience 3-time stood for perfection. In the classical era, in which the harmonic and tonal apparatus was accorded high place in music the key of C major was a paradigm of the highest excellence. The notion that this key was a kind of *virgo intacta* among keys lasted for a long time.

Within C major, the "perfect" key, Mozart wrote his final manifesto on the nature of symphony, with reference in the second subject of the first movement to comic opera and in the last movement to the great traditions of polyphony that he had absorbed not only from the north German school but also from the great Bolognese teacher, the Padre Martini. The C major symphony, "Jupiter" only because of the whim of some unknown admirer, defies all kind of verbal explanation. It is a summary of the human condition solely in a medium of communication that here may seem absolutely self-sufficient. This, perhaps, is really what absolute music is: certainly, and this symphony is the great example, absolute music is not music without awareness of the humanism which was the inspiration of the modern European tradition of music.

While Mozart's career thus proceeded, meteorically, that of Haydn was following a more or less measured course. Mozart, intense, nervous, sensitive, in later years was the ideal of the artistic temperament. There are at least three German novels about Mozart (the most famous being by Mörike), in all of which virtues apparently not of this world are ascribed to him. Of all composers he is the one who, to the laity, was immaculately conceived and born without artistic sin.

With Haydn it is otherwise. He is the benevolent father-figure – the "Papa" Haydn of legend. He had the advantage, of course, of outlasting the appointed span of the Psalmist. Now, Mozart was urban, metropolitan, and ambitious. Haydn, on the other hand, was never more happy than when out of city life and closeted with his friends or members of his family in one of the numerous (still excellent) public houses of Eisenstadt. A man of pawky humour, which was made the more redolent by the dialect which he neither shed nor wished to shed, he was without enemies. His only cross (as he put it) was his ill-tempered, neurotic, wife; whose function however, was effectively supplemented, at one point of his life, by the singer, Luigia Polzelli.

The personality of Haydn, as thus we know it, is evident in

his symphonies. Particularly the later symphonies, in which his own genius had been further stimulated by that of Mozart. By 1788 Haydn had composed just about twice as many symphonies as had Mozart. In that year he wrote three (nos. 90–92) for a Count d'Ogny. (In the next year he sold them "exclusively" to another Count, and then made an extra profit on them by disposing of them to yet another patron anxious to ride to posthumous glory on the reputation of Haydn.) The third of the symphonies – all of which are suffused with a Mozartian sublety of modulation and instrumentation – was played in Oxford in 1791 when Haydn was awarded a Doctor's degree, and is thus distinguished as the "Oxford" Symphony.

It will not fail to be noted that 1788 was the year that preceded 1789. This revolutionary year also made a convenient point of division in the history of music. As has been seen the symphonies of Mozart had by this time been written. Those of Haydn which came after 1789 were those on which his fame as a symphonist largely depends.

Although he was all for the quiet life, Haydn, in middle life, was a European celebrity. He had written commissioned works for Cadiz (*The Seven Last Words*) and for Paris (of which the most familiar is the symphony "La Reine", no. 85 in B flat major), and published works in various countries. In the 1780s most European musicians of eminence found it profitable to visit London. A first attempt to induce Haydn to come to England was made by the Earl of Abingdon in 1784. In 1789 John Bland, the publisher, went all the way to Eisenstadt to try to persuade Haydn to sign a contract. Two years later, somewhat more free in respect of his Esterház duties on account of the death of Prince Nicholas Esterházy, Haydn made the long journey to London, his sponsor being Johann Peter Salomon, promoter of the principal symphony concerts of the period.

On March 11, 1791, Haydn made his debut as conductor (directing the music from the piano) at a Salomon concert, and the second part of the concert opened with the first performance of a new symphony, no. 96 in D major (the "Miracle", so-called). Haydn won ready sympathy from the public by his ease and charm of manner. The orchestral players, true to an abiding tradition, not only liked but also respected him since, vastly experienced, he knew precisely what he wanted. He was (although never satisfied with the amount of time available for rehearsal – a perpetual complaint) able to inspire playing the like of which had hitherto rarely been heard in London. The first performance of Symphony No. 96 was made unique by the fact that the slow movement was encored.

Haydn's first visit to London inspired the composition of six new symphonies (nos. 93–98). In 1794 he returned for a second round of engagements. In between these two journeys to London signs of a change in the balance of power were apparent. Mozart had died at the end of 1791, and in 1793 a young Rhinelander (who had been present in Bonn when Haydn was received there with affectionate respect in 1790) became a pupil of Haydn in Vienna. This was Ludwig van Beethoven – a young man of the new age, revolutionary by temperament and conviction, and anti-establishment.

The second London visit of Haydn occasioned the composition of six more symphonies (nos. 99–104). These included the "Military" (no. 100 in G major), the "Clock" (no. 101 in D minor-major), the "Drum-roll" (no. 103 in E flat major), and the "London" (no. 104 in D minor-major). These works were the climax of Haydn's symphonic career, and the summary of a lifetime's experience.

In principle these works observed the canons of the classical period, but, even more than the symphonies of Mozart, they exemplify the comprehensiveness of the aesthetic of the period. Having established the viability of formal procedures Haydn left them as guide-lines. The least dogmatic of musicians, and one who was most responsive to the communicative potential of music, Haydn left the symphony open-ended. Each of his symphonies has its own distinctive character, and no two are alike. Symphony no. 98 is dignified, even austere; Symphony no. 104 is spacious and even-tempered; the slow movement of no. 98, an *adagio*, has an ethereal Mozartian beauty, and the subtleties of Mozartian melodic inflection are found in all the late symphonies though not always in obvious contexts; the variations of the "Surprise" and the "Clock" are emblematic of the pawky, ingenuous humour, of a Burgenlander, though in the former are signs of the stresses and storms that Haydn observed in the affairs of the age. Signs of tension are also apparent in the changing function of the minuet. What had been a relaxation – a reference back to Arcadia, or to the nearer bucolics of the Austrian countryside – became a vital instrument for the propagation of the dramatic. In symphonies 99 and 104 Haydn's adventurousness brought new shades of meaning to the minuet, while in the latter the fast tempo lands the minuet on the threshold of the Beethoven scherzo.

Mozart was critical of society. Haydn was tolerant of its foibles. Beethoven was intent on changing it. Whether Beethoven was capable of formulating a coherent social philosophy is doubtful. What he could do was to shatter the existing conventions concerning the nature and scope of music, and from them fashion new ones. In respect of the symphonic music of Mozart and Haydn the listener may well feel that the music is congenial on account of the ideal quality with which it is invested. Since both composers observed certain restraints – and to this extent exemplified a classical sense of propriety – they seem to be at one or two removes from the stresses of our age. Patently these are eighteenth century composers and modern interpretation often makes this abundantly clear. Perhaps, when over-emphasing the *galant* virtues, too clear. In the case of Beethoven, however, the image is different. The music of this master, often born of distress and protest, is much more in line with contemporary feeling. Mozart and Haydn were both accustomed to a little world. True they pushed far beyond its limits, but none the less the sense of limitation remained. They – even if disliking the thought – were servants of their masters and of their public. Beethoven regarded his mission not as that of a servant but of a master. This point is surely made in the opening of the "Emperor" Piano Concerto.

That he became the great master of the nineteenth century was due to his absorption of techniques and principles and to his application of these to fresh intentions. So far as actual melodic contours, harmonic groupings, contrapuntal gestures, and even instrumental practices are concerned, Beethoven wrote relatively little that would have been found exceptional in the final Haydn-Mozart era. He did, however, break beyond discretion in the matter of rhythm, introducing a percussiveness (intensified by drums, and on occasion other untuned percussion) that must once have seemed atavistic and primitive, in pushing the limits of general tonal and dynamic contrast further away from each other, and in expanding the whole scale of symphony.

In respect of Beethoven the term "classical" acquires a new significance. That he was heir to the classical precepts of the eighteenth century is clear enough (in the first two, and the eighth symphonies, as well as in the piano sonatas and chamber music up to, say, the appearance of the "Rasumovsky" Quartets (Op. 59), but this kind of hereditary involvement with classicism *per se* is less important than Beethoven's extension of the inherent principle of comprehensiveness. The term "classical" is attached to Beethoven as it was attached to Goethe, and this, paradoxically, means that the fact that he was a Romantic, in one sense, increases rather than diminishes the classical stature. It has already been stated that music is the consequence of a relationship between composer and audience. Beethoven intuitively and accurately appreciated the feelings of those who, emerging through the maelstrom of Revolution and Napoleonic Wars, lived in a new state of spiritual insecurity and reached out for the certainties implicit in the ideals advertised in the newer philosophies. On the one hand, therefore, we discover a new belief in the potential of the individual and in the perfectability of society, on the other a faith in the recreative capacity of Nature.

Beethoven's reading of the heroic lives in the "Eroica", but also in the music for the ballet *Prometheus* (of which a theme from a *contre danse* motivates the last movement of the "Eroica"), for the overture and incidental music to Goethe's *Egmont*, for the overture to Heinrich von Collin's *Coriolanus*, and in *Fidelio*, with its three attendant *Leonora* overtures. The progress of these works is one of optimism, in that their general termination represents the eventual triumph of positive over negative, major over minor, good over evil (the terms are interchangeable). Tension is expressed in the contrarieties of colour, tonality, melodic contour, tempo, dynamic, and, above all, rhythm, with which Beethoven invested the sonata form (whether in overture, symphony, concerto, pianoforte music, or any other form of chamber music). The summary of aspiration is the best of the symphonies, the Schiller-inspired "Choral Symphony", which by being so (the choral movement is the finale) either renewed the spirit of the early Baroque *Symphonia* or fractured the classical concept of "symphony". At any rate, beyond this point symphony was never again the same.

It is equally true of the concertos (five for piano and one for violin) that stand firm in the standard repertoire. The piano concertos inaugurated a new era of relationships within the concerto partly because of Beethoven's appreciation not only of what the piano was but what it was to become (i.e. the dominant voice of the individuality of the Romantic composer), partly because of the enforced reassessment of sonorities introduced by the nineteenth century orchestra, but largely because Beethoven expressed his own personality most effectively and most dramatically by way of his own performance. Dramatic is the operative word, as is evident at every turn; in the vital rhythmic pulsation of the Third Concerto, in the immediate entry of the solo instrument (an introductory orchestral *ritornello* having hitherto been the custom) in the Fourth Concerto, in the prodigious vistas opened up in the Fifth Concerto, and in the tremendous significance attached in all to contrasts between movements. The urgency of Beethoven's thought is most succinctly and emotively expressed in the famous drum beats that herald the Violin Concerto. At such moments we are reminded of the fundamental fact that awareness is primitively stirred by the quickening of the pulse. Rhythmically, Beethoven put the clock on by putting it back, by re-exposing the primitive urges that were to become part of the "classical" principle of the twentieth century.

The apothesis of melody that is the Beethoven slow movement – the consequence of the fusion of Italian and German principles of song within that of sonata-style development – on the other hand is a reflection of the impulse of wonderment.

73

This same impulse is the source of the symphonies of Schubert. So long as attention was focused on the heroic and philosophic content of musical works the symphonies of Schubert were held in lesser respect. Schubert the great song-writer could not have been a great symphonist. Q.E.D. Part of the problem lay in the relative or absolute unfamiliarity of Schubert's larger works. The eighth of Schubert's symphonies (the two-movement "Unfinished") was written in 1823 – for the Styrian Musical Society of Graz of which Schubert was elected an honorary member. It was first performed some fifty years later, the score having been put aside and forgotten by the Director of Graz. The Ninth Symphony (the "Great" C major) was not performed until after its discovery by Mendelssohn more than a decade after the composer's death.

The symphonies of Beethoven retain their hold because of their power. Those of Schubert on account of their beauty. Within the Romantic period the personality of the composer became a potent factor in the general appreciation of the public. The *persona* of the composer prior to the nineteenth century had signified relatively little. During the nineteenth century it became all important. Thus the divergence of musical works from a hypothetical norm, helped on by the increase of virtuosity in every field, spelled the end of classicism. Beethoven was one end, but also a beginning. By the same token Schubert (whose classical aims are condensed into the Fifth Symphony) was also an end and a beginning.

5

Romantic Music

ONE may work backwards from this one. There is no doubt as to what kind of, so-called, "classical" music is most popular. It is that which lies in the area marked off at one end by Peter Ilyich Tchaikovsky, and at the other by Beethoven – the Beethoven of the post- "Eroica" phase. The "Eroica" was an explosive work, bred in violence. The last of Tchaikovsky was the Sixth, "Pathetic", Symphony which ends in darkness, despair, and death. The two terminal points of nineteenth century symphony, thus boldly epitomised, provide a clue to the character of the music of an epoch. This epoch was, of course, not entirely enclosed, and the prevalent moods extended beyond the convenient date-line provided by the death of Tchaikovsky and the almost simultaneous impact of his last work on the world. There are notable out-liers of the post-Napoleon nineteenth century ethos of symphonic music in Mahler, Sibelius, and Elgar.

Although the works so far indicated may be accepted by the public at large as "classical" they should, more precisely, be defined as "romantic". In the case of Beethoven, however, we are on unsure terminological ground, for he, as has already been stated, is both classic and romantic. This suggests two conclusions: that, like Monteverdi, Beethoven lived at a time when attitudes and techniques were changing, and with them the communicative properties allowed to music; and, again like Monteverdi, that he saw the past and present (and, maybe, the future) as one entity. Both conclusions are correct, and, in turn, give a hint as to the essential nature of musical genius.

From the information already available in the preceding paragraphs some idea of the fundamental and general character of Romantic music may be gained. The "Eroica" Symphony represents an attempt to elucidate the meaning of the "hero" concept. Beethoven, admiring the revolutionary Napoleon (as, I think, any servant of a reactionary German Court of the eighteenth century was entitled to do) intended to use music as a fitting means of paying tribute to a great man. His original intention – to dedicate the work to Napoleon – was frustrated when Napoleon forsook the pure principles of revolutionary thought and became Emperor. Beethoven did not approve of Emperors. He tore away the Dedication of the Symphony which he sent into the world as an elucidation and symbol of his own idealism. Music, being less earth-bound than any other art, is the only medium through which ideals in an abstract form (and ideals being what they are must always remain abstract) may effectively be set out. This brings us into the realm of metaphysics. A metaphysical influence was strong in the development of nineteenth century music.

"Music," wrote Beethoven to Bettina Brentano, "is a higher revelation than the whole of wisdom and the whole of philosophy . . ." Running all the way through Tchaikovsky's thoughts, and finding outlet in the programmes – both implicit and explicit – of his works, is the word *Fatum*. Fate, destiny, what you will, carried almost every major composer of the nineteenth century into realms of musico-philosophy hitherto unconsidered. When Brahms's Third Symphony was first performed on December 2, 1883, the principal critic of that time in Vienna rehearsed his conclusions not only on this but also the previous two symphonies. "In his C minor Symphony," he wrote in the *Neue freie Presse*,

Brahms plunged, with the very first dissonant bars, into despairing passion and gloomy Faust-like speculation; the Finale, reminding us of the concluding movement of Beethoven's 'Ninth', in no way changes, with its tardily achieved reconciliation, the essentially pathetic, nay, pathological, character of the composition, in which a suffering, morbidly – excited individuality finds expression . . . Brahms's Third

Symphony . . . repeats neither the mournful song of Fate of the First nor the joyous idyll of the Second; its fundamental tone is conscious, deed-loving strength . . .

That is the measure of the change in musical attitudes brought about by Romanticism. The terminology, the probing seriousness, the psychological enquiry, would have usually raised a guffaw in the eighteenth century (among composers at least) when the composer was a craftsman and knew the limits beyond which music should not go.

By convention, however, classical music was allowed to be representational. Aspects of nature were admitted as suitable stimulus even to a symphonic composer. But the "hunting" symphonies of Haydn, the "Turkish" symphony of Romberg, the "Battle" Symphony of Neubauer were regarded as no more than superficially illustrative. The emotional states exhibited through the apparatus of *opera seria* were emotional states of heroic, but mythological, characters. The fact that we choose to interpret the music of Gluck, or of Mozart, with hindsight should not allow us to ascribe to them ideas which are ours rather than those which were theirs. The classic case of misrepresentation, of course, is *The Magic Flute*, which started as a popular comedy, and grew into a ritual.

The change which made possible our present attitudes (speaking in general, and on behalf of the mythological norm of the "music-lover") took place during the Beethoven period. This is when Romanticism took hold. What has been indicated above as a new, philosophic approach to music had many facets. Overall, was the concept of music as a symbol – a symbol of "a higher revelation". The two poles of this "revelation" were the natural and the supernatural. So far as the natural was concerned this meant a new twist to humanism. There was man in his social environment; there was man in his natural environment: on the one hand, man and man – or man and woman; on the other, man and nature.

Now the "Eroica" shows Beethoven's regard for the extraordinary man – the superman. It also exemplifies the composer's attitude to the flawed superman, the hero who at the end fails on account of preponderant faults. Whether or not this is written into the music is arguable (what is the funeral march there for?), but it is certainly contained in the familiar story of the mutilated Dedication. A classical composer would have left the Dedication and kept his thoughts on the situation to himself. A composer of romantic temperament, inspired by the immanence of the ideal, could not easily do this, for his attitude towards his vocation was quite different from that of his predecessors. The romantic composer was no longer prepared to think of himself as in an inferior station. He was the arbiter at least of beauty, and he himself was a hero, or of heroic stature.

The hero motiv, with its new connotations, runs through romantic music. The "Eroica" at one end of the period is complemented by another "Eroica" at the other. Elgar's Second Symphony is a tribute to the heroic principle, which inspired him through a large number of works, of which the planned but unwritten "General Gordon" symphony is the most relevant. Musically and psychologically the connection between Beethoven and Elgar was by way of the hero-obsessed Wagner.

A believer in Romantic principles, however, was obliged to extend the concept of the hero. From Jean Jacques Rousseau there derived the comforting thought that every man was, or, at least, potentially was of the stuff of which heroes are made. The end of this was the optimistic acceptance of the eventual perfectability of, and brotherhood of, man. It was only under such conditions that composition of a Choral Symphony, culminating in a setting of Schiller's *Ode to Joy* was possible. It was only under the impact of such a faith that Mahler's Eighth Symphony could have been conceived. This symphony, writes Hans Redlich, contains a "passionate appeal to the godhead for the granting of universal love." It will be noted in passing that both Beethoven's Ninth and Mahler's Eighth Symphonies are works of great dimensions.

A consequence of the large-scale philosophy was the assembly of large-scale forces to express it. That we are now less likely to think this way should not be permitted to obscure the nineteenth century aesthetic tenet that there was a link between size and profundity. The Romantic period was the period of the large orchestra, as also of the large choral society. If Berlioz had not written a *Messe des Morts* someone else would have done so. If Mahler had not come up with a "symphony of a thousand" one would have been provided by another hand.

The many-sidedness of Romantic humanism stemmed from the hero principle and led to the great climatic of universal brotherhood, and (what is the same thing) universal love, and also to a closer analysis of the human situation not only as it might be, but as it was.

The antithesis to the extraordinary man is the ordinary man. The nicest tribute to the ordinary man, and the ordinary woman, is wrapped up in Elgar's "Enigma" Variations. Apart from the immortality conferred by sets of initials, or well-understood cryptograms, inscribed above the respective movements, who would know anything of B.G.N., "Dorabella", "Troyte", "G.A.S.", or even "Nimrod". In the "Enigma" Variations we have extraordinary music inspired by ordinary people, much to be preferred to ordinary music inspired by extraordinary people.

If the antithesis to the extraordinary is the ordinary then that to the hero is the anti-hero. The Romantic period saw the musical apotheosis of Manfred (Schumann and Tchaikovsky), Don Juan, Don Quixote, and Till Eulenspiegel (all Strauss), and, in many forms, Faust. The latter, indeed, is a crucial figure in the mythology of the Romantic era, whose character as delineated by Goethe variously affected Beethoven, Schumann, Wagner, Liszt, Gounod, Spohr, Busoni.

The true anti-hero of the nineteenth century was the subject of the Fantastic Symphony – that is himself as seen by Berlioz. So far as symphonic music is concerned this is the yard-stick by which Romanticism may be judged. A vital work in any consideration of music it is unique in that it could only have been created when it was, that is in 1830.

The composer of the classical era was a professional (except for the occasional aristocrat who composed as a hobby.) That this should have been the case was inherent in the social function of music, which imposed on the creative musician a whole range of practical activities. In the Romantic period the non-professional composer came into his own. Non-professional, perhaps, requires definition. The implication is that it was no longer absolutely necessary for one who aspired to creative activity also to act as Kapellmeister or Kantor, or to sell himself to the public as a virtuoso performer. The increasing complexity of music in any case made it difficult for a man to cover many fields (even though Mendelssohn so successfully did), while an upgrading of the creative process encouraged a belief that a degree of detachment – sometimes leading to virtual alienation – was desirable in an artist. Of the greater musicians of the nineteenth century Berlioz, Schumann, and Wagner, were, in the narrower sense, non-professional, in that none of them served what hitherto had been considered the proper apprenticeship. But they were neither unprofessional nor amateur in accomplishment. That this was so was due to their capacity for enlarging the semantics of music, and necessarily altering structural conventions, so as to make it a vehicle for the emotional and spiritual aspirations of the age in which they lived.

For the lesser musicians of the classical era music was something of a closed shop. The production of symphonies by minor figures – like Vanhall, a particular favourite – was more or less according to stereotype. The form became an end in itself. It should be clear, of course, that restrictive practices applied only in the case of lesser composers; but, since there are always a proponderance of these, it may be realised that their influence was out of proportion to their quality. Now Berlioz, in particular, detached from the professional conventions was able at first to look at the field of music from the outside.

The son of a doctor, and himself intended for that profession until discouraged by a revulsion at the sight of blood, Hector Berlioz, so far as music was concerned was largely an autodidact. He entered the Paris Conservatoire at the age of 23, and, essaying larger projects than his techniques admitted, failed to achieve the coveted Prix de Rome until 1830. Formative influences were the French Romantic movement in literature, the fiery, exciting performances of the orchestra of the Société des concerts du Conservatoire, and, especially, the interpretation of Beethoven's symphonies by François Habeneck. All these influences helped to ignite a combustible imagination. Berlioz, whose literary talents were hardly less than his musical talents, saw that the proper course for music to take was towards, and beyond, the aims of literature. The leap from the Beethoven type of symphony to a new kind is defined in a letter which Berlioz wrote in February, 1830, to Humbert Ferrand: "I was about to begin my symphony in which the development of my passion will be depicted . . ."

There is passion in Beethoven, but of a general nature. In the case of Berlioz the passion was particular – for Harriet Smithson, an Irish actress. Apart from a love affair that pursued an uneasy course, Berlioz at this time was obsessed with other difficulties. He was financially insecure, and making little headway career-wise. In such a state he prepared his autobiography – but in terms of music. The *Fantastic Symphony* was the result.

This is avowedly programme music. The titles of the movements are here sufficient to indicate the composer's intention, though the titles were expanded into fairly detailed annotations which were handed out to an unbelieving audience when the first public performance of the symphony took place. The subject of the first movement is "Reveries and Passion," of the second, "A Ball," the third is entitled "In the Fields", the fourth "March to the Scaffold", the fifth "The Witches' Sabbath".

Immediately the break with tradition is indicated by the provision of five movements. The first movement, slow introduction followed by an *allegro* – which, however, is also *agitato*, follows in the main classical procedures. The second movement is a waltz – brought into vogue after the Congress of Vienna in 1815 – and this concession to popular taste indicates a further shift of symphonic direction away from its aristocratic antecedents. At this juncture we may as well refer to the thematic interdependence of movements. The object of the composer's affections (Miss Smithson) is represented by a theme (an *idée fixe*, later to be Teutonised as *Leitmotiv*) of sufficient independence of character readily to be recognised at any point in the course of the work despite the changes involved by the different environments in which the theme was to be placed. In one form or another the *idée fixe* is to be heard throughout the *Fantastic Symphony*.

The personalisation of the symphony as well as its generally programmatic character impelled Berlioz to work not only through structures, but also through sonorities which were both novel and indicative. In the third, pastoral, movement (with the storm and peace after the storm already familiarised by Beethoven) the actual sounds – as particularly of cor anglais and of the four timpani – are in themselves significant, quite apart from their structural relationships.

The matter of sonority increases in importance with the impact of the concluding movements. The "March to the Scaffold" was, and for all I know may remain, a horrific experience for the listener brought up on a conventional diet of the classics. Why a march to the scaffold? The artist had, in his dream, killed his beloved. In the final movement of the *Fantastic Symphony* the triumph of the forces of evil is portrayed in a cataclysmic demolition of the plain-song theme "Dies irae" by orchestration that was as eccentric as it is exhilarating. The real victim sacrificed on this particular scaffold was "good taste". This in the long term had an emancipating effect, the results of which are to be seen in the blood and thunder of later Romanticism which, Zola-wise, turned eventually into Realism.

The *Fantastic Symphony*, a work of the senses, was sensational and so it remains. It is not difficult to see to what extent it illustrates tendencies which have run through into the present day. There are certain aspects of this work which, since they have a general significance, require underlining. First, there is the quality of introspection which encouraged a new attitude to the purpose of music. After Berlioz the habit of attempting psychological disquisition in terms of music became more frequent. Since Berlioz himself acknowledged the force of Goethe's *Faust* it is not surprising that introspective tendencies developed in Germany and Austria. The main vehicle for these was the *Lied*, and the influence of the *Lied* on German and Austrian composers from Schubert to Richard Strauss was immense. As a consequence of the intense subjectivity indicated by Berlioz, and also by Schumann, it is not surprising that the dominant trait of later Romantic musical philosophy is pessimism. The spread of pessimism is one of the least encouraging features of nineteenth century music, and its results are apparent not only in the symphonies and symphonic poems of Tchaikovsky (who was much impressed by Berlioz when Berlioz visited Moscow in 1867) but also in the first phase of Schoenberg.

The *Fantastic Symphony* is an exploration of the subconscious. It is, in fact, the record of a dream. The way into this uncertain sphere was by way of realism. But at the end there opened out a grand vista of the unreal. The half of Romantic poetry and music is concerned with the dream state, and titles of works all along the line indicate the fascination which this field held for Romantic composers. The greater religious works of the period – the Masses of Berlioz, Verdi, Bruckner, and so on, are now no longer adjuncts to liturgical necessity, but expressions of submission of will to the myth of Christology. The end of the Romantic road of dreams is, of course, on the one hand, Elgar's *Dream Children*, on the other, *The Dream of Gerontius*.

In these two works lies yet another Romantic concept (borrowed from age-old mythological and religious contexts): of purity and purification. To place these terms in opposition to the "evil forces" and processes of corruption written into Berlioz's Symphony (as also in the various presentations of the *Faust* legend) and to give musical references is, perhaps, doing no more than re-stating the obvious end of sonata procedure – the contrast of two themes. But, once again, the intention of the Romantic musician was to be specific. The theme of purification (the subject of Wagner's *Lohengrin* and *Parsifal*) was symbolised in various ways, most clearly by the Gretchen figure out of *Faust*. That of purity, by way of Rousseau and Wordsworth, led to an idealisation of childhood. The child as a musical emblem first comes into consideration in the nineteenth century. The *Scenes of Childhood*, and other such collections, by Schumann and other composers, although laudably created in order to supply practical needs, were in a sense idealisations. The idealisation of the child state of innocence is variously exposed at the end of the nineteenth and the beginning of the twentieth century. As, for instance, in the last movement of Mahler's Fourth Symphony, when a soprano voice expresses the presumed delight of the child over the heavenly entertainment novelettishly laid out in an indifferent poem taken from *Das Knaben Wunderhorn*.

This Fourth Symphony of Mahler, was described by Donald Tovey as a pastoral symphony; as to the opening of the symphony he referred (from the promontory of a professorial Chair) to its "farmyard noises". Here is a point at which to rest and take stock.

As is now becoming apparent, the Romantic composer was pulled in two directions. Idealism led him towards the absolute (poets and painters followed suit in endeavouring to incorporate the allusive qualities of music within their own arts), towards the paradisal regions indicated explicitly in, say, the conclusion of Schubert's *Die junge Nonne* at one end of the era and the Second, Third, Fourth, and Eighth of Mahler's symphonies at the other, and, implicitly, in almost every symphonic slow movement of the period. César Franck's D Minor Symphony is a *locus classicus* in the sphere of Romantic musico-philosophising, not by its intrinsic character so much as by the legends accumulated about the "seraphic" personality of the composer and by the description of the main theme of the slow movement (warmed up by the distinctive colour of cor anglais) by Guy Ropartz as the "motiv of Faith".

All this aspiration towards the ideal gave a new twist to a much-abused word: "beauty" became an end in itself, an end approved both by artist and public. It is the word which occurs most often in the writings of Tchaikovsky and Elgar, both of whom were obsessed by the thought that beauty might perish from the land. Neither of these composers was definite as to what beauty was. The best that can be done to construct an aesthetic principle from stray comments is to suggest that they saw in the corpus of traditional music values and modes of expression a spiritual validity that led them to take up the position of defenders of the faith against iconoclasts who threatened from positions of extreme nationalism or of technical heresy. The general public approved the citation of beauty as an ideal and placed it above and away from actuality. But the public pursuit of idealism increasingly became a process of escape. Escapism became a dirty word; by the time it had arrived in the vocabulary, however, music had taken another turn in order to escape from the charge of escapism.

While musicians wandered off towards the Elysian fields they were also nagged by the claims of reality. The polarity of music is, of course, in-built, and the tension between the ideal and the real is no more than an actualisation of – and – or classical and romantic, or, for that matter, sacred and secular. The contrast became more positively expressed in the nineteenth century to accord with the expansion of interest in ideas and in music, and as a result of a more wide-ranging musical terminology and the creation (as by *Leitmotiv*) of a convenient set of references for the listener. The most effective agent for the dual purpose of exploring both the ideal and the real was the enlarged orchestra.

In the first place one considers the latter process if only because it then seemed (and still does to the general body of audiences, it may be suspected) of first importance.

The whole apparatus of orchestral sonorities, as developed in the nineteenth century, was geared to the business of showing things as they were. The history of the orchestra by and large, is part of the history of the art of musical representation as primarily practised in the theatre. The record of Romantic orchestral music is written in a long list of descriptive titles, and extensive programme notes. The programme note writer is hard put to it to elucidate the G minor symphony of Mozart in narrative terms (not that the attempt has not been made). But – with the help of Schumann – he can go a long way towards plotting a weekend tour through the Saxon countryside through Schumann's "Spring" Symphony.

We are now placed within a naturalistic framework of which the supports, so far, are Beethoven's "Pastoral" Symphony, the slow movement of Berlioz's "Fantastic" Symphony, Schumann's "Spring" Symphony, and Mahler's Fourth

Symphony. In the classical period a detached view of nature obtained. Certainly it was there, but was all the better for tidying up. The formal garden of the Mirabel Schloss in Salzburg (still as it was) was what nature should be disciplined to. As for the rest the phenomena of nature which admitted of it were legitimate subjects for discreet imitation. Beethoven was content to follow classical principles in designing a "Pastoral" Symphony, and the naturalism of the work – bird-calls in the slow movement, an energised scherzo to indicate the storm, and so on – is superficial. Beethoven himself, though a new-style nature-lover with an appreciation that led towards mysticism, emphasised the point rather carefully by issuing the statement that the symphony was "more the expression of feeling than painting." In the case of Berlioz there is an assimilation of man to nature; the contrasts of the *Scène aux champs*, musically more realistic and painterly than those of Beethoven, are also the indication of personal moods.

Schumann's First Symphony was composed some ten years after Berlioz's "Fantastic" and was first performed in Leipzig in 1841. Here, for the first time in symphonic movement, we encounter the true Romantic spirit fully absorbed. The work is avowedly literary, being an exposition of a poem by Adolph Böttger. It comprises the customary four movements, advertised respectively as "Spring's awakening", "Evening", "Merry Playmates", and "Spring's Farewell". This symphony takes up the descriptive practices of Weber and amalgamates them with those inherent in the *Lied*. Schumann was, of course, one of the greatest song-writers and the distinction of his instrumental works lies almost entirely in his re-statement of the lyrical qualities of the *Lied* in instrumental terms. The "Spring" Symphony is a *melodic* Symphony. Schumann knew the limits beyond which music should not go in search of realism and thus provided the ideal symphony for his age. It does not need here to be said that the poetry that inspired the German–Austrian *Lied* of the Romantic period was essentially lyrical, and that the lyrical impulse derived from opening the windows on the world of nature. Through the open window each man saw what he would, so that the pastoral influence broadened –

eventually ending in the Impressionism that became a fresh point of departure.

Schumann, whose inner life was one of dramatic conflict, found nature on the whole a therapeutic agent. So also may we. The Fourth Symphony – the second to be written, also in 1841 – is stronger than the First, with finely gauged contrasts of major and minor tonality, of rhythmic figuration, of homophony and counterpoint. The resolution of the work, however, lies not in the *Triumphlied* of the last movement, but in the serenity of the second movement, the *Romanza*.

The "serenity" of nature – a gift from the poets – became in itself a Romantic *idée fixe*. It is apparent in the symphonic work of Bruckner, Dvořák, and Mahler, and in non-symphonic works by almost every popular composer of the nineteenth century. The Fourth Symphony of Bruckner (the "Romantic") is an enchanting lyrical survey of Austrian landscape from the point of view of a dedicated Catholic. This symphony (published in its full version in 1889) is descended from Schubertian principles on the one hand and from Schumannesque attitudes on the other. Part of the charm of Schumann consists of his naïve allusions to bucolic activity (in the Third Symphony the peasants make merry on the banks of the Rhine). This same kind of irradiation of landscape occurs with Bruckner, whose third and fourth movements of the Fourth Symphony are peopled with "merry peasants".

In the course of time folkiness gave a bad name to Romantic music, but Bruckner, Schumann and Dvořák, may be exonerated from it. Bruckner and Dvořák especially, like Haydn from whom also they could claim musical descent, knew peasant life, because they were, and were not ashamed of being, of peasant origin. Dvořák is, perhaps, first choice for the "natural man". The most ebullient and conversational of nineteenth century composers, he summarised the principles of Romantic symphony to perfection in his Eighth Symphony in G major (op. 88). While he was working on this symphony, in 1899, Dvořák was mostly living in the country, at Vysoká, in Bohemia. As much as possible he spent his time in his garden, which, he said, he loved "like the divine art itself".

At this juncture we note that Dvořák was not only a composer; he was a Czech composer. And this fact assumes a considerable importance, which is exposed in the chapter following. The interest in nature in general led to an interest in locality and this, combining with other factors, gave rise to the nationalist branch of Romantic expression.

Nationalism in its purest sense belongs to vocal and choral music, and to opera, more than it does to purely instrumental music, which is more likely to give an illusion of nationalism – at least of overt nationalism. It is, for instance, difficult for the casual listener to disentangle the authentic from the un-authentic – the *Slavonic Dances* of Dvořák, for instance, from the *Hungarian Dances* of Brahms, the *Spanish Dances* of Falla from those of Moskowski, the "Irish" music of Stanford from that of Bax. I stress the casual listener as distinct from the connoisseur or the student, and take the opportunity of remarking that in the long run, in the post-classical era, it is the casual listener who seems to have ultimate control. For reasons which are not far to seek, and which will be more fully explained, the casual listener reaches out towards any form of artistic expression that appears to carry an aura of mystery. It is, indeed, the listener and not the musician who lives in the ivory tower, and so long as he does the composer will nourish sufficient of his illusions to keep him there. The unbeliever comes near to belief when he hears the great examples of church music; the staid and inhibited find relief in musical glosses – say by Berlioz, Tchaikovsky, and Prokofiev – on the loves of Romeo and Juliet; any music with a topographical label stirs the imagination even before the music is heard. One end of enjoyment lies in the exotic. The exotic element, appearing in many forms, is the dominant factor in music of the Romantics.

In earlier periods, exoticism was pursued for its novelty. The topographical references in Wilbye's *What needeth all this travayle?* or Weelkes's *Thule, the period of cosmography*, have no correlative musical gestures. The Chinese Dance of Purcell's *Fairy Queen* is strictly, and engagingly, European. The ballet of Savages in Rameau's *Les Indes galantes* is urbanely panto-mimic. While the percussion of the "Turkish" music of Gluck and Mozart does little to stimulate credibility. In the Romantic era, however, the exotic was pursued for its own sake – either to shock or to please. In some cases the pursuit of the exotic represented a form of protest on the part of the composer.

An appreciation of the wilder aspects of nature was urged on by prevalent attitudes in literature and painting at the beginning of the nineteenth century. It was in response to such trends that Mendelssohn composed, for example, the marvellously evocative "Hebrides" Overture, and, somewhat later, Rimsky-Korsakov the marine music of the Symphonic Suite, *Scheherazade*.

One should bear in mind that it was during Mendelssohn's lifetime that Scotland became generally fashionable as a distant subject for romantic contemplation. Not least was this due to the wide-spread enthusiasm for the poetry of Robert Burns (the inspiration of many song-writers, including Mendelssohn, Schumann, Robert Franz and Reger among the Germans, the Hungarian Mihály Mosonyi, and in our own time, Dmitri Shostakovich). Mendelssohn, an indefatigable tourist, made a broader survey of Scotland in his Third Symphony in A minor, in 1842. For the idea of his Fourth Symphony, in A major (written some nine years before the Third), Mendelssohn drew on his enthusiasm for Italy, and this symphony – incorporating a slow movement "pilgrim's march" and a *Saltarello* as finale – is both a masterpiece of painterly musicianship and a wonderful attraction to the arm-chair traveller.

In one way or another Italy inspired the affection of almost every Romantic. Three other works come to mind: Berlioz's *Harold in Italy* composed at about the same time as Mendelssohn's *Italian Symphony;* Tchaikovsky's *Caprice Italien;* and Elgar's *In the South*. The first of these, a symphonic work with an important solo part for viola, has a literary origin – in Byron's *Childe Harold* – and a relationship with the *Symphonie Fantastique*. In place of a march to the scaffold, however, there is a pilgrim's march (second movement) while the conclusion represents an orgy not of witches but of brigands. It will be noticed that marches, whether of pilgrims or others, assumed a higher importance in the Romantic era; partly because of their associative value, partly because military pageantry – a spur to nationalism – was enwrapped within the Romantic spirit and partly because of the influence of opera and ballet on musical thought in general. Tchaikovsky's brilliant *Caprice Italien* was mostly composed in Rome in 1880 and is a quodlibet of Italian folk-songs, brilliantly scored. Elgar's *In the South* – written in place of a promised symphony for the Leeds Festival of 1904 – goes one better than Tchaikovsky's Caprice, for in place of folk-song it carries what Elgar separately issued as a *Canto popolare*, an *ersatz* folk-tune about the provenance of which the listener, carried away by the sheer loveliness of the scoring, is indifferent. So, no doubt, he is to Elgar's literary aids to inspiration, which included Tennyson, Byron, and Virgil.

Tchaikovsky, although a strong patriot, was under no illusions about the quality of Russian Czarist civilisation and he was continually unhappy about the restrictive actions of an absolutist government and the philistinism of much of the middle class of Moscow and St. Petersburg. The fact that his music looked towards France and Italy brought some criticism in Russia and more in Germany (where it was assumed that the more like German music it sounded the better every other kind of music was); but his proclivities in this direction stemmed not only from a recognition of artistic virtues but from a taste of alienation from some aspects of Russian life. In somewhat similar manner Elgar, whose feelings about the lack of encouragement given to artists in England were strong and frequently expressed, also sought sanctuary abroad from time to time. Somewhat earlier than *In the South* he wrote the engaging set of six part-songs (of which three form an independent orchestral suite), *From the Bavarian Highlands* – a most attractive memento of a summer's holiday in Garmisch.

Apart from Italy, the Slav countries, Switzerland, and Scotland, the happy holiday hunting-ground of the Romantic composer was Spain, and Spanish dances (or pseudo-Spanish dances) found their way into the concert-hall and the drawing-room through evocative colour-prints by Lalo (*Symphonie espagnole*), Moskowski, Elgar, Saint-Säens, (an orchestral Barcarolle seductively entitled *Une Nuit à Lisbon*), Rimsky-

Korsakov (*Capriccio Espagnol*), and in the post-Romantic period, by Debussy and Ravel. At a later point came the Celtic impressions of Arnold Bax, and others.

Meanwhile – and this belongs to the succeeding chapter – the geographical veracity of Romantic music was being strengthened by overt nationalist gestures, by the incorporation of less familiar types of folk-song into the traditions of overture, symphonic poem, symphony, and so on. Thus the explorer, in musical terms, was pushed into further regions: Saint-Säens composed a *Suite algérienne* in 1879, a Fantasia for piano and orchestra, *Africa*, in 1891, and in 1912 the middle movement of a *Triptyque* for violin and piano was a "Vision Congolaise".

The fictional quality that developed in the concert music of the nineteenth century stemmed on the one hand from the primacy of the novel and the general popularisation of literature (which, of course, radically affected opera), and on the other as a reaction against the increasing claustrophobia induced by industrialisation and urbanisation. Since this claustrophobia remains for the greater part of the populations of the "advanced" countries so too does the wish to escape from it. Hence the enduring attraction of Romantic music which, in offering at least temporary release from the immediate processes, remains the solid core of the repertoire.

6

National Music

IT IS, I hope, by now clear that music – more than any other activity – cannot be sorted into categories, like goods in a department store. It is only a kind of balance of payments system that enables us to do this up to a point – admittedly a point of convenience. The following pages could quite well have been included within the preceding chapter; but I give way to the legitimate inclinations of the day-dreamer. National music became an issue during the Romantic era, but it had, of course, existed long before, even though not always acknowledged as such. In Germany, indeed, the idea of nationalism in music preceded that of nationhood.

At the present day the significance of national music rather depends on who you are and where you are. In an "emergent" nation, or a resuscitated nation, or a nation which, having undergone violent revolutionary changes, is attempting to rediscover its own identity the mention of national anything is expected to send the pulse-rate up. I have heard African music in the middle of Africa, Bohemian music in the middle of Bohemia, Slovenian music in the heart of Slovenia, and Magyar music among the Magyars. In every case the existence of a national idiom in music, the reconstitution and extension of a definite tradition is not only an article of political belief, but incentive to a sense of communal responsibility. In Britain and America we do not see it that way, though gestures in that direction have by no means been unknown and the possibilities of tutored introversion are not altogether remote. The reassessment of Elgar, on the one hand, and – more surprisingly – of Charles Ives on the other, is not quite unconnected with tendencies towards a renovated nationalism.

On the inside one sees a spate of collected editions that testify to the zeal of musicologists, but also to the necessity for putting as much as possible in the national shop-window. There are, then, splendid opportunities for cultural window-shopping. This is the innocuous position of the dreamer that is in all of us. The persistent amateur of music who is stirred by the topographically appropriate sleeve design of Smetana's *Ma Vlast* or Sibelius's *Finlandia* is likely to be affected in a similar manner by the music that lies within the sleeve. The impressions received from exposures to such music are not dissimilar from those which are activated by the holidays abroad pictorial guide issued as a magazine supplement. One sort of music that is within the general category of national music thus represents one aspect of the Romantic ideal, but brought down to ground level. A composer who avowedly composes nationalist music does so because he considers that his own country either is or ought to be a heaven on earth. There is a great danger that the process ends in a singular, and embarrassing, naïvety. There is a dismal catalogue of "folksong suites" that can be compiled from any country; but since the majority of such suites pass rapidly out of circulation the task is of no more than narrowly academic significance.

Nationalism has inspired a great deal of indifferent music. It has also inspired music without which we should be the poorer. And the whole of music has benefited from the terms that have come into general usage from within some national context or other. Practically the whole of Russian music stems from nationalism. Without this as foundation Stravinsky would not be one of the dominant voices in twentieth century music. The magic of Bartók is the consequence of national loyalty (a loyalty severely strained by the circumstances of his life), while the music of Sibelius, Vaughan Williams, Falla, Shostakovich, Aaron Copland (to name but a few) is distinctive on account of the concern of these composers with the ground-roots of local music and/or with the condition of the society to which they belong.

It may well be that the average music-lover comes in at this point – with a natural interest in the qualities and idioms of national music – and that this chapter should have been introductory. But the situation is more complicated than it appears. What, after all, is nationalism; and what becomes of nationalism when it is distilled into the abstractions of tonal structures? That the issue became a significant one during the Romantic era is due to a collusion of circumstances, to an efflux of philosophical and political ideas on the one hand, to the expansion of musical vocabulary on the other.

Because music is always more than music the impulse which we now define as national was always implicit. Thus folk-songs and folk-dances were localised from the start by subject and by association. In the case of folk-song – taking it all the way up to the ritualised songs of more or less developed societies; that is hymns and national anthems – it is clear that a particular loyalty was stimulated both by the character of text and by the fact of possession. A blind belief in the superiority of one's own folk-songs to all others is, even now, by no means unknown. So far as dance is concerned, psychological importance formerly reposed in the dramatically symbolised actions to which, at first, music was accompaniment. The acknowledgement of the pre-existence of significant dramatic conflict is acknowledged subconsciously when we are stirred, for instance, by Borodin's *Prince Igor* dances, or by the *Dances of Galanta*, of Kodály. The distinguishing feature of folk-music is rhythmic. Folk-song is affected by the laws and patterns of speech, folk-dance by the manner in which inborn physical tendencies which have been co-ordinated into group movement are regularised and synthesised.

In the formative period of western art music folk-music was shoved across the side-lines. First, the Church – an international institution – aimed at a musical conformity that, when achieved, became one of its most remarkable accomplishments. Second, the ruling class of aristocracy – its security only ensured by the maintenance of social structure in which the gulf between the lower and the higher orders was rendered unbridgeable – encouraged a type of music that gave the appearance of exclusiveness. "Classical" music may very well appear to be the best music: once upon a time it was made for the benefit of the "best" people. In the small world of Europe the best people, in this sense, made a select, but international, set. The *concerti grossi* of Corelli, or Vivaldi, were composed by Italians under Italian patronage, but they were not composed for the Italians. They were composed for the entertainment of a privileged minority. The same applied to the symphonies of the Mannheim and early Viennese composers. Even more did it apply to the chamber music of, at any rate, pre-Beethoven days. The assumption of the less privileged (not yet extinct) that such music was for "them" and not for "us" was well-based, even if the refusal to come to terms with the situation as it now is seems unwarranted.

The strains that we now recognise as national come into view at different times to act as a corrective to the attitude of ex-clusiveness. The common man and the art of the common man, never out of sight but often assumed to be, infringed on the art of the uncommon man during the Renaissance period to some effect. The chorale, on which the victory of Lutheranism was based, was the apotheosis of folk-song. Some chorales were folk-songs; others were adaptations of melodies that had come to have the validity of folk-song. The chorale was the foundation of the music that we still recognise as distinctively German. The difference between the German Bach and the de-Germanised Handel lies in the fact that to the one the chorale was, and to the other was not, immediately relevant.

The chorale was not consciously nationalist. Unconsciously, however, there was no doubt about it. Its absorption into the music of the Lutheran liturgy was facilitated by the particular circumstances of the German States. The Lutheran was an Erastian Church; the acceptance of a national ideal based on home, and hearth, and language, was common both to princes and peasants; the church cantata, as composed by Telemann, and Bach, and Graupner, and a hundred other composers, held a great deal more significance than its music alone suggested. On the whole one does not refer to the nationalism of Bach (Germany did not then exist, but the idea did) because such reference seems irrelevant. Alternatively, since the manner in which he exhibited national (i.e. local territorial) themes was on the grand scale it appears impertinent. Besides, at the back of one's mind runs the impression (however falsely based this may be) that music is in some way or other "universal". Nonetheless, from the beginning of the nineteenth century the German-ness of Bach was fully explored, and exploited, and he was turned into one of the father-figures of the German nation.

J. S. Bach, however, was not one man but many. In apposition to the *St. Matthew Passion* we may set the *Peasant Cantata*. In the proper sense the former is a tragedy; the latter is a comedy. The comedy consists of a contrast of manners. The laugh, a kindly one, is on the peasant – symbolised by the thick, ungraceful, dialect of the Saxon, and the folk-melodies that at some point or other had grown out of and enveloped this dialect. The peasant, or the simple man ("simpliccisimus", in fact), had for a long time had his place in folk-drama, and in the often extemporised performances of the strolling-players, and, when he was brought into the court play, or the university diversion, he was a figure of fun. But once the real peasant, as opposed to the Arcadian abstraction, appeared in art he was difficult to get rid of. What some thought nonsense, others considered sense.

The creative musician, of perception, was well-placed to recognise such sense where it was evident in musical terms. Not long after Vivaldi had enshrined the fastidious Ovidian concept of Nature in "The Four Seasons", Telemann was sitting in a draughty pub in Sorau in Poland, listening respectfully to the crude music of the peasantry. "One can," he said, "hardly believe what wonderful ideas such pipers or fiddlers have when they improvise while the dancers rest ... A careful listener could get enough ideas from them in a week to last a lifetime." The way in which Telemann introduced Polish impulses into his music is one of the more striking features of Baroque music. Dance movements overtly acknowledged this influence (particularly the Polonaises of the Suites), but Polish rhythms spread throughout larger works – as the *Concerto Polon* or the *Sonate Polonaise* – so that in this, as in other ways, Telemann brought, as Romain Rolland said, "some fresh air into German music."

So far as Telemann was concerned his appreciation of national idiom sprang from two sources; from an atypical indifference to distinctions of rank (as a young man he composed music for miners' festivities) and a warm-hearted concern for human beings, and from an awareness that all that glittered in the music-rooms of polite society was not music. Telemann had an ear for the exotic and his incorporation of exotic elements into the standard structures of the Baroque allows us, at least, a double portion of exoticism. Let it not be forgotten that one of the principal attractions of "national" music for us is the opportunity it affords to indulge our taste for what appears as safely unfamiliar.

The type of music that comes from any composer is conditioned not only by what kind of composer he is, but also what kind of man. If we accept, as I think we should, that the art forms created by a man are also the man himself, then the circumstances from which he emerges become germane, certainly to understanding, and, in the long run, to appreciation. For the plain man (and also for the not so plain man) the figures of composers preside over the impressions received from their works: Who is not affected by his image of Handel, or Bach, or Beethoven? Or of Haydn?

In popular imagery the shapes of such masters are much distorted. This is particularly the case with Josef Haydn. We should, of course, suspect that the urbanity that is often accepted as a dominant characteristic is not the most important factor of personality. He was a classical master by courtesy of classification, but another view would show him as a great disturber of the equanimities. Haydn, as a child, in remote Rohrau (and it is still remote) was brought up to one kind of music – the music of the peasantry. By the due processes of education he was made to accommodate himself to the artificialities of formal musical expression. But, being an honest man, he did not try to cut himself away from his roots. One of his notable contributions to musical thought was to practise the principle of non-divisibility. The search for new sonorities (which we see as the process of settling the proportions of the classical orchestra) was a response to the memories of rural music; much as at a later point in time was that of other composers whose origins were in the same area of Europe: e.g. Liszt, Dvořák, Kodály, Bartók.

Sonorities – although we may now see them isolated in modern techniques – coexist with forms, particularly when they occur in uninhibited folk music. Haydn picked up the musical phraseology of the Burgenland (and brought it into the ambit of urban music). There may be instanced the last three movements of the String Quartet in D major (Op. 20, no. 4), the last movement of the String Quartet in C major (Op. 33, no. 3), the second and third movements of the Piano Sonata in D major (Hoboken, XVI, 37), the second movement of the Symphony in E flat (no. 103), the interesting and provocatively forward-looking *Zingarese* for piano of 1799, and, of course, the popular "Gipsy" rondo – *rondo all' ongarese* – of the Trio for violin, cello, and piano in G major (no. 25).* Such reflections on the unconventional – which brought imbalance and eccentricity into the classical field – bespoke an affection for a fundamental pattern of life to which Haydn reverted whenever possible, but also a sense of pride in its certitudes. Since neither the Hungarians, nor the Croats, nor the other ethnic groups who comprised the community into which Haydn was born enjoyed any national status, other than that imposed by decree from Vienna, and within the fictitious domains of the Holy Roman Empire, Haydn could hardly be termed a nationalist composer. But he helped to chart the way which more self-consciously nationalist composers of later date might follow.

Haydn lived across the French Revolution and into the Napoleonic Wars, both of which brought a new dimension to the shape of nationalism. As is well known the Emperor's Hymn (the basis of a typical set of variations in the String Quartet in C major (Op. 76 no. 3), and therefore known as "The Emperor"), composed by Haydn, was a symbol of Austrian identity, and the popularity of this work gave incentive to composers elsewhere. In the post-Napoleonic period nationalism took more aggressive form.

In search of unity the Germans built up the great composers of their tradition – Bach and Handel – into *national* heroes. The "heroic" as more abstractly discussed by Beethoven, was

*To this aspect Hungarian musicology contributed much.

98

narrowed down to local-heroic proportions and then blown up into a concept of a particular national entity. This is best appreciated in the mass of male-voice choruses composed by both major and minor composers in great numbers for the *Liedertafel* societies (male voice choirs) that sprang up everywhere. The effects of German politico-philosophical nationalism are felt in almost every musical work of German origin written during the post-Napoleonic period. The "Reformation" and "Rhenish" Symphonies, by Mendelssohn and Schumann respectively, are perhaps more aggressive than outwardly they seem. The former, centred on the chorale "Ein fest' Burg", which is the foundation of the fine finale, is an apotheosis of the historic mission of the German nation within the religio-political sphere. The latter – in its fourth "Cathedral", movement – refers to this mission more allusively and more mystically, but in general terms picks up and expatiates on the virtues of a national way of life. In both cases the message is clarified by the headlines; in the one case these consist of the direct quotation of a familiar melody well sanctified in the national *mythos*, in the other by the useful rehabilitation of Bachian (i.e. "German") counterpoint, and by the patent bucolics of the second movement. The intention that lay behind such music is to some extent covered up by the quality of the music – it is often further hidden by the character of interpretation – but it is not to be forgotten.

In an article on the Danish composer, Niels Gade, Robert Schumann described a process of disintegration that appeared to be taking place in the 1830s. "Things begin to look," he wrote, "as if the nations bordering on Germany wished to emancipate themselves from the hegemony of German music. This might annoy a chauvinist German, but it could only appear as a natural and cheering phenomenon to the profound thinker and the student of humanity." Schumann noted the patent urge towards national expression in the works of Chopin, Sterndale Bennett, Verhulst (a Dutch composer), and the Scandinavians, Lindblad and Ole Bull, as well as Gade.

In some cases nationalism showed the exploitation of folk-music – as in the *Polonaises* and *Mazurkas* of Chopin – who was stirred to protest through a revolutionary fervour that burst into revolt in Poland in 1830; in others it was a matter of atmosphere. By reason of "its lakes, mountains, runes, and northern lights", the Scandinavian composer was urged to consider that "the North might well be allowed to utter its own tunes among those of the world". Note the use of "be allowed" – an unconscious sign of Schumann's innate belief in the superiority of German method, which is also evidenced by another remark on the composers above mentioned: "But since all these composers seem to regard Germany as their first and favourite teacher of music, no one will be surprised that they try to speak their own musical language to their own nations, without being untrue to their former instructors". The limitations thus imposed on musicians who sought to express the powerful impulses that often moved them as individuals, added to the not infrequent inhibitions caused by political considerations (especially in the field of opera), meant that the process of emancipation was a gradual one.

The nineteenth century composer aimed at freedom, of one sort or another; but he could not go very much faster than his patrons allowed. Generally free from the incubus of aristocratic patronage, he was now under the supervision of the "public", basically a conservative public, with a firm belief in the virtues of picturesque romanticism. Music of "national" character (and the nationality did not always matter all that much) was welcomed in the concert-hall because it was romantic, because it was made intelligible by means of programme annotation. The art-collector of the Romantic period preferred a picture with a story. To satisfy this preference painters in all countries showed a business-like zeal. The same applied in respect of music.

There are many facets of nationalism in art, and there are of Romanticism, of which in any case nationalism is a derivative. National art may be ritualistic; it may be symbolic; it may be positive, and aggressive towards other national groups; it may, on the other hand, be positive, but seeking to redress inner imbalances; it may be, as in latter-day English or American nationalist art, theoretical; or, of course, all these facets may be combined. The pulse stirs at music patently inspired by national motivs, particularly when these spotlight the exotic properties of unfamiliar melodic formulas or when fresh and stirring rhythmic features are exploited. Nationalism moved in music in the nineteenth century for three reasons.

The drive towards naturalism led to an appreciation of landscape; not landscape in general but that to which one was attached by accident of birth. Landscape also meant the people whose customs, dress, and speech, were seen as distinctive features grown from and entirely associated with landscape. So much is clear in Schubert's warm-hearted settings of Wilhelm Müller's lyrics, in the pastoral images in Berlioz's landscape movements, in the merry peasantry of Schumann's cheerful Rhineland sketches.

A new turn to nationalism came with a realisation that the peasantry was not as it was supposed to have been from time immemorial. That the idyll was but an illusion, and a dangerous illusion at that, brought out a new realism. Behind Russian liberalism, in particular, there grew the conviction that national greatness depended on emancipation of the peasants, or a more equitable social organisation. International music, that is German and Italian music, with their conventions, was but a support to the establishment. The massive originality of Glinka, Balakirev, Borodin, Mussorgsky, Dargomizhsky, Cui, and Rimsky-Korsakov, developed from resistance to established conventions, to a reverence for the fundamentals of musical expression and national legend, and under the impulses that started with the Decembrist uprising of 1825 and spread across the century until they reached the grand climacteric of 1917.

The emancipatory aspect of nationalism was twofold. First, it enshrined the doctrine of the liberation of the underprivileged (to whom was accorded a special designation of nobility not, perhaps, always warrantable); second, it held the thesis of national independence. Naturally, the two were often conjoined. This was particularly the case in respect of the composers of the countries of eastern Europe, where, to some extent, the same attitudes are still promoted.

The power of musical nationalism at one time is a sign of the communicating virtue that European music once possessed. That it is now less communicative by function is due to the rapid development of other forms of communication that, overriding frontiers, are more immediate in effect. The bardic faculty of the musician was still possible to exercise up to the time of the First World War; since that time it has fallen into abeyance. This is one cause of the confusion in which the twentiety century composer finds himself.

The ritual value of music is appreciated most fully in a religious context. With the decline of purely religious doctrines and the rise of secular philosophies (nationalism was one) that impinged on and sometimes destroyed them, ritualism in music – which had come by way of folk music and its magical properties into the ambit of religious experience – became transferred to a secular sphere. Hence Wagner turned the opera-house into a temple, and the concert-hall became a kind of shrine. The panoply of the Czarist Court, the mystical influence of the Orthodox Church, an intense devotion to the idea of the fatherland, and the new devotion of folk music, stimulated an enormous output of ritualistic nationalist music in Russia. There were, for instance, Glinka's *Kamarinskaya* (based on Russian themes), and Balakirev's *Overture on Russian themes* and the Symphonic Poem *Russia*, which was in effect a second overture on native melodies. The most evident example of such music, however, is the "1812" Overture of Tchaikovsky, a superb occasional piece and (whether one approves it or not) a marvellous apotheosis of a national hymn.

The ritual of nationalism, similarly expressed in unmistakable and popular terms, is also to be observed in such works as Dvořák's *Hussite Overture* (composed for the opening of a new National Theatre in Prague in 1883). The significance of this work lies in the citation of parts of two chorales – "Ye who are God's valiant warriors" and the St. Wenceslaus Chorale – of which the first was also used by Smetana in the two final sections of *Ma Vlast*, and the second in instrumental works, by Josef Suk and Vitězslav Novák. Ritual music is, of course, more commonly associated with words (there is a large pile of national cantatas, now long forgotten, belonging to every

European country and to America, that were composed during the latter part of the last century), and instrumental music that belongs to this class strongly implies an accompanying text. Certain incidental music (not to mention opera and ballet) goes into this category; for example Grieg's pieces for Ibsen's *Peer Gynt*.

In the case of what may be termed symbolic nationalist music it is much more a matter of atmosphere than of narrative. In this the symphonies and symphonic poems of Tchaikovsky, Dvořák, Sibelius, and Elgar, return somewhat to the intentions of Beethoven's "Pastoral" Symphony in registering impressions rather than in painting pictures. One may adduce another factor that draws each of these composers into spiritual compatability with Beethoven; each one, while conscious of his status as a citizen of his own country was also concerned to live out his own individual life through his music. The classical properties of symphony were the yardstick against which each measured himself; national idiom or atmosphere as absorbed into his artistic consciousness was the means whereby he could establish his own independence, even when availing himself of the traditional techniques. The end of the exercise, however, was not to provoke a minority response (as within one national group), but to address the world at large. Tchaikovsky was a zealous collector of folk-music, and folk-tunes are to be found in plenitude in the symphonies (especially the Second), and in the Violin and First Piano Concertos, and the character of the instrumentation is often seemingly an idealisation of folk-music sonorities. But when Tchaikovsky's melodies were original they often showed features otherwise to be found in folk-music. As in Tchaikovsky so in Dvořák it is often impossible and always unprofitable to attempt to delimit the influence of folk-music. As did Tchaikovsky with Russian, so did Dvořák grow up with Czech folk-music, with the result that he became part of it.

We are here brought up against an important question, that is less easy to answer than it seems. What, in fact, is folk-music? Elgar once gave a brusque response to this. "I," he said, "am folk-music." And he did not mean this arrogantly. He, correctly, saw the nineteenth century composer living and working in an urban and advanced society as the heir to the bardic traditions and duties. With that simplicity that is one part of his greatness he assumed that some part of his task was to inspire his compatriots – not some of them, but all of them. In the obvious sense he more than did this through the vivid, but varied, textures and moods of the *Pomp and Circumstance Marches*. Quite clearly these, or at least, the first and fourth, have been assimilated into the national consciousness to the extent that they exercise a strong emotional effect even on those who are unaware of their provenance. As near as makes no odds they are, then, folk-music. Like that of Elgar the music of Sibelius is, if not folk music (for he was not in the habit of quotation), of the folk – by common consent. *Finlandia* (a tone-poem) centres on a hymn motiv that has taken the place in Finnish culture of the most evocative chorales in that of Germany.

The end of folk-music, as its beginning, as Kodály pointed out, is not its particularity, but its universality. Thus, passing by the clearly jingoistic, we arrive at the point where nationalistically inspired music becomes international. The end of this is the "New World" Symphony: Czech or American-negro? It is, of course, both, and both the fierceness and tenderness which are the emotional extremes of the work have no narrow significance. The "New World" Symphony is a symbol of hope for the underprivileged. The point was recognised at an early date, and was not always appreciated, as is suggested by a programme note of a London Promenade Concert in 1901.

"About nine years ago," the anonymous writer stated, "Dr. Dvořák settled in New York as Director of the National Conservatory of Music . . . and several of his most recent compositions . . . are based on themes in which he has imitated the peculiarities of the American negroes' 'plantation' melodies and the songs of the Indian tribes. These, he asserts, should form the basis of a national American music. His view is, naturally, not universally endorsed – indeed it gave offence to many Americans; but it contains undoubtedly an element of truth that should not be overlooked."

The "New World" Symphony is a synthesis; of ideas promoted by two indigenous musical idioms that are made to become one. (This is the natural end of folk-music, as it was its beginning; since the basic formulas of primitive melody appear to be the same the world over.) The idioms, however, are absorbed into the imagination of a composer, whose technical accomplishment was achieved by way of mastery of the *lingua franca* of European music, particularly Viennese music, during the Brahmsian era.

As a composer Dvořák shared with composers like Elgar, Richard Strauss, Tchaikovsky, Sibelius, and every other late Romantic, the intention to express himself. On the whole, that aspiration is now often hidden from sight; to which the listener may have some justification in observing, "the more's the pity!"

The nationalism of the nineteenth century artist was a matter largely of intuition. In the twentieth century, in so far as nationalism has continued to exercise influence on musical behaviour, the tendency has been towards scientific evaluation. In a deliberate way such masters as Vaughan Williams and Kodály have evolved their individual idioms from an intensive scrutiny of folk-music characteristics, and also from a reconsideration of national cultural patterns in wider fields. In neither case, however, has the scholar been allowed to subdue the passion for causes that characterised each man during his lifetime. Vaughan Williams, like Elgar, had a deep concern for the wider cultural traditions of English life, a mystical sense derived from the philosophies of the poets (*The Lark Ascending* is clearly a "poetic" work, and may so be felt), and from the English Church, and a liberal outlook on social and political questions. In the end, perhaps, it is the mystical quality in Vaughan Williams that abides. Monuments to this sense of mystical apperception are the *Tallis Fantasia* (the mysticism is implicit in the basic tune by Tallis himself) and the Sixth Symphony, of which the vanishing *Epilogue* represents one of the more sublime moments in English music. There is, however, a hard edge to Vaughan Williams's mysticism. Not given to over-elaboration of statement (this is the point of departure from the later phases of German romantic-classical expository method) he went straight to the heart of a problem, with a bluffness that may be said to stem from the pragmatic instincts of the English. The most striking example of the plain-spoken Vaughan Williams is the Fourth Symphony, a study in discord that has often been interpreted as a commentary on the social and political discords of the 1930's, when the work was conceived. Vaughan Williams himself gave no support to this kind of interpretation.

In the case of Kodály the urge towards a national idiom (which in the end became a very personal one) was fired not only by a love of the past, but a deep concern for the present and the future, and by the ideal of national liberation. The theme of liberation is embedded in hundreds of choral works, particularly the *Psalmus Hungaricus*, but also in instrumental works. Of these the most impressive is the highly original "Peacock" Variations, in which the implications of the poem of the song are worked out through rhythms and sonorities that stem from the wide Magyar traditions of song, ritualised folk-drama, and rural entertainment, and of history. In this work one notices in particular how much the details of instrumentation contribute to the overall impression. The "about-ness" of the music is enhanced by the divisions of the strings, the incisiveness of the upper woodwind, the irradiation of the harp, and so on. Here, we say, is an evocation of the countryside around Lake Balaton.

Which takes us back to one of the starting-points. Music affects the imagination not only through the ear but also through the eye. This, perhaps, implies illusion. One asks, therefore, is "national, or nationalist", music an illusion. In some ways it is – except in specific cases where external factors count for more than music itself – for unless instructed we are hardly aware, when listening, of geographical particulars. On the other hand the character of music warms our sympathies, towards the composer as a man, and, maybe, towards the composer in his environment. In the end we remain grateful that nationalism (less destructive in effect in music than elsewhere) has broadened the resources of music. It has been the great agent in the popularisation of the art, and this was one of the causes of nationalism anyway.

7

Modern Music

"MODERN MUSIC", collectively speaking, is a rude word much used by the cautious as a prophylactic against incaution. Non-swimmers are well advised not to throw themselves in at the deep end of a swimming pool; but the analogy, although often employed, is invalid in respect of the arts. Especially in respect of music, and more especially in respect of private musical experience of the individual listener. Prejudice (and there is plenty of it) against so-called modernity in the arts as often as not is the result of conformity to a public prejudice, which is directed less against the arts than against other aspects of social behaviour. Oddly enough, the attitudes which the layman, overweighted with the opinions of others, decries within the arts are those which, privately, he would wish to adopt as his own. The operative word is freedom, here to be qualified as freedom from conformity.

In theory, at least, modern music – in the sense of contemporary, or near-contemporary – should be the starting-point for musical experience. This should be the music with the most meaning, with the greatest relevance to modern life and thought. Indeed, like the music of every other age that of the present time is reflective – of ways and thought, of trends in the allied arts, of social circumstances, of technological progress – but the listener frequently prefers to turn his back on it. Or, more precisely, he likes to think that he does.

There are a number of reasons for this. Principal among these is the unwarrantable assumption that whereas almost everything else is getting better and better (optimistically defined in the phrase "rising standard of living"), music (in the upper appreciation bracket) is getting worse and worse. Now such quantitative calculations may be relevant in respect of the productive and distributive methods of, say, tooth-paste, but are hopelessly irrelevant if applied to what are piously, but not improperly, termed "works of the spirit". They only appear to work by a blatant disregard for the facts.

The not uncommon prejudice against modernity is usually built on a system of faulty premises. I hasten to add that many of the sponsors of modernity are equally capable of negligent reasoning. But, as will be seen, this is by no means a new phenomenon. The antagonists, however, tend to place themselves in a position of dialectical weakness. It is well known that the most vociferous opponents of modern music are those who have not listened to any. By-passing that we come to those who, standing in perplexity, are led astray by conventional errors of opinion or judgment.

Modern music, by those whose proclivities are in the direction of the "classical", is used much too exclusively. Thus it is taken to signify music of advanced techniques emanating from the so-called "western" world. A revolution spells contemporaneity, but a counter-revolution may do exactly the same thing. The significance of either depends on where one happens to be standing. Next, there is an unwholesome tendency (in process of correction by certain shifts in critical opinion and critical status) to examine modernity as such solely within the context of "serious" music. It is an odd paradox that in popular music (i.e. "pop") what is not contemporary is as ill thought of as what in "serious" music is. The tiresome thing is, of course, that "serious music" has to be dragged in by the tail, an exercise that was not formerly necessary. A historian considering, say, the Baroque era studies, or should study, the whole range of musical activity of the period, recognising that the only valid categories for critical classification are – good, bad, indifferent. These three categories still stand. Alas, by what standards do we judge? Here we are thrown back on a list of expedients which lack general significance.

In former times one pushed aside works because they lacked formal propriety, and even if the requirements of formal purpose were less than they sometimes appear to have been in retrospect we knew what we were talking about. In short, we meant repetition, and development, of thematic material, and a convincing set-up of complementary tone-structures categorised as movements. At the other end of this came the call for variety. Monotony was a non-virtue. Monotony comprised two aspects, both of which stemmed from a lack of musical inventiveness. A symphony by, say, Vanhall would now arouse little enthusiasm (though this was not always the case) because, in comparison with Haydn, it would explore the obscurer rhythmic and harmonic channels with, to say the least, extreme circumspection, while in overall intention it would stick fast to the abstracted prescriptions of formal behaviour laid down by the academics. Vanhall followed fashion. At this point it may be observed that it may be just as disastrous to follow a "progressive" as a "conservative" fashion (the two always co-exist) too slavishly.

At the present time there might appear to be almost as many fashions as there are composers. If this were true, and if it meant that composers had achieved the ultimate in individual freedom then we should rejoice. But the appearance is deceptive. The fashions boil down to a number of recognisable modes of intention and procedure. Intention gives us what we have had before. There is the intention of entertainment – wrapped up most demonstratively in the generic term of Beatle-music, and not much less demonstratively in the currently popular "musicals". On the other hand there is the intention of functional efficacy, which leads to a wide range of productions ranging from liturgical music of various kinds to radio, television, and film scores by way of works contrived (as, patently, in those States where Marxist-Leninist philosophies impose specific doctrinal considerations) for reasons of morale-boosting. In between comes a large supply of allegedly abstract music.

In theory, liturgical music is bound by certain extra-musical considerations that affect the nature of the music. The same obtains in respect of the "applied" music of the socialist systems. In both cases the principle is that of intelligibility. Leaving these branches of music on one side for the time being we look at the central core of modern music to discover that intelligibility still counts as a criterion; even when perversity leads to unintelligibility being acclaimed as the same thing as intelligibility.

We have been here before. For various reasons I am always inclined to boost the claims of Georg Philip Telemann to be included in the top twenty. Those who share with me an affection for his music (such as is recorded, and it is very little in relation to the whole corpus of his output) will, no doubt, be surprised to discover that he was in one place and in respect of one work, at least, regarded as well beyond the permissible frontiers. In one of his church cantatas – *Beware of false prophets* – he went through a complete cycle of tonalities, each one being distant from its predecessor by the interval of the fifth. Taking into account the nature of the text – and the title is sufficient guide for those disinclined to refer to the First Epistle of *John 4*, 1–3 – the tonal activity is seen to be not only programmatically effective but also logical. Just as logical as is a contemporary essay in serial technique. The Cantata was first performed in the city of Erfurt and as it happens the circumstances of the first performance were detailed by the excellent writer, Jacob Adlung. The work, believe it or not, was performed without rehearsal, by singers and players whose knowledge of the theory of music was slight. After the performance, said Adlung, those who had been present asked one another what the music was all about. "But," he continued, "it was too late for asking questions!"

The situation is similar to one in which the reader may very well have found himself. Telemann confused the musicians of Erfurt in about 1744 by *technical* departure from the norm, which led to unusual relationships of sound-groups. The illustrative principle that he was following was, however, the very foundation of that type of music. In this instance Telemann was operating within narrow limits, and the consequences of such experiment had little general significance.

Rather more than a century later the progressive principles of Richard Wagner were much more upsetting. No doubt we have caught up with them now (though in regard to the totality of Wagner it is to be doubted) but even at the end of the nine-teenth century there were many who spoke as trenchantly on Wagnerian as some may now speak on Schoenbergian theory and practice. In 1876 Tchaikovsky complained that *The Ring* was "boring", that the vocal parts were "colourless", that the harmonies were "muddled", and that if this was the music of the future he was not much in favour of it.

Tchaikovsky – superficially, by popularity ratings, the plain man's composer *par excellence* – here gives an undeniable exposition of the plain man's reaction to "modern" music in general. In fact, the sum total of his critical asides, as collected from his correspondence, add up to a jeremiad. He was more than critical of the Russian nationalists, he took a grim look at Brahms, and despatched the young Richard Strauss with some contempt. He adored Mozart and Bizet, and welcomed Grieg and Rachmaninov. In Tchaikovsky's eyes the music of Mozart represented the zenith of civilised expression – and his love of European values, as opposed to Russian values, was based on their higher content of tolerance and free expression. Bizet, as represented by *Carmen*, had a vitality and zest that he found therapeutic. So far as Grieg was concerned, he admired the freshness of outlook that came from a non-doctrinaire percep-tion of the invigorating qualities of folk-music. Rachmaninov, of course, seemed to be an heir-apparent – a point not lost on those acquainted especially with Rachmaninov's Piano Con-certos. That the pattern of Tchaikovsky's approval is erratic serves, on the one hand, to exemplify traits of personality, and, on the other, to demonstrate the fallibility of human judgment in these matters if infallibility is to be ascertained from the apparatus of appreciation that arrives with hindsight and not always at first sight.

Having thus far appeared to have dealt somewhat peremp-torily with Tchaikovsky it is only fair to amplify the bare statements by reference to his reasoning. The difficulty with modern music in Russia, he wrote to Mme. von Meck on July 18, 1880, was that it was a conflation of

spicey harmonisation, extravagantly original orchestral

combinations, and all sorts of superficial effects. The musical idea has been pushed into the background. It has become not the aim but only the means; that is, the reason for the invention of this or that combination of sounds. This purely brainy [i.e. "intellectual"] process of musical reasoning makes contemporary music, however amusing, witty, curious, and even "tasty" (an expression invented by and characteristic of the new Russian school) at the same time cold, not warmed by real inspiration.

Yet, within that lies the fact that Tchaikovsky as a composer was frequently himself regarded with suspicion on account of his compositional attitudes. In Moscow and St. Petersburg he was by many and for most of his life seen as one who revelled in obscurity. In France it was said that he was too German; in Germany that he was too French. He himself, in a not infrequent moment of despair, wrote that he anticipated that his time "would come in the future".

The future, so far as Tchaikovsky is concerned, being here we can, in fact, appreciate that his prognostication was accurate. The so-called present "classical repertoire" is engagingly full of works that, had the majority opinion at the time of their first production been sound, should not be there. Tchaikovsky shrewdly opined that when technique became an end in itself the long-term prospects were poor, and that when the "musical idea" was reduced in potency there was a danger of atrophy. It is on this that the present argument still hinges. But what is the "musical idea?"

To this there are a hundred different answers, none of which are more than fractionally satisfactory. There are, however, two familiar lines of thought that may once again be examined. The "classical" argument carries us along a logical road; the "romantic" argument along that of intuition. In contemporary terms we may follow the former in any one of the vehicles of musical formalism. This brings us by way of the neo-baroque, of Hindemith, and the neo-classical, of middle period Stravinsky, or of a small symphony – the "classical" – by Prokofiev so advertised, and the pseudo-science of Schoenberg (the 12-note principle being based on faulty premises in acoustics, and, therefore, inductive logic) to the argumentative exercises of Webern and the post-Webernians. While the processes thus hastily observed may go beyond the limits of the "ordinary listener" it should be said that by opening up new vistas of sonority disposition they have helped to liberate the composer. A generation ago a young composer was still learning his craft by reference to the formulations of theorists brought up to an inflexible belief in the motions of classical style. Living, as we do, in a traditional era, it is difficult to see what comes when the patterns are brought together and united in a new classicism. That is, if this happens. In a transitional period we are also obsessed with the application of the prefix "neo" to many familiar phenomena. For instance, "neo-romantic."

The "romantic" strain in music, so far from being dead, has never been so alive, and if a rearguard action is being fought at all it is being fought by the neo-classicals. The leading neo-romantics, Messaien and Orff, for example, concerned with fundamentals, are all in favour of renewing the textures of music from the resources of what is still exotic (i.e. Asian or African folk-music, or, in the special case of Messaien, bird-song). Exotic in this connection tends to elevate the ideal of the primitive, and in this connection what is medieval, although far from primitive in one sense, is taken to have the virtues of the primitive in another. The pungencies and (musically speaking) naïveties of Orff's *Carmina Burana*, a series of medieval secular poems set in quasi-medieval manner, are a case in point. The popularity of *Carmina Burana* reposes in the fact that it appeals to, awakens, and partly satisfies, the primitive in all of us.

We now begin to see some sort of framework about which we may assemble the pieces in our own repertoire. If the framework will also be found to accommodate non-contemporary music, so much the better. The time-chart is a frequent deception. The wise listener regards every piece to which he listens for the first time as modern – to the extent that it is unfamiliar, and, in being unfamiliar, provocative of thought. Modernity, in fact, is a matter of experience.

Sufficient has been said to make it clear that there is no such single entity as "modern music", but that there are a variety of aspects of musical thought which may be distinguished as moving away from the accepted norms of yesterday. Just as there is no "modern music" as such so there is no one progenitor of what is thought to be "modern". In any case, candidates for this title tend to be shuffled round by the *cognoscenti* to suit their own theories of the moment.

What we look for first, perhaps, are the liberating influences. The legend of classical music that is commonly held is in itself constrictive. The break-out from the formal limitations of the legend was, as has been seen, more or less ostentatiously achieved by Berlioz less ostentatiously by Schumann, who for long was in England the *enfant terrible* of music. The Second Symphony, according to the *Manchester Guardian* of December 29th 1865, was "vague and unsatisfactory" ... there is an abundance of pretty phrases, but they are fragmentary and do not belong to any central unity". Approaching the problem from a somewhat different angle further dissolution of classical principles was stimulated by Wagner and Liszt. In respect of Wagner, however, it may be said that his achievement was to reintegrate the elements of music rather than to introduce new ones. Avowedly he turned opera into the more cohesive music-drama to which he gave symphonic purpose. By destroying the supremacy of the Italianate vocal line, and by equalising the contributions of voice and instrument he not only diminished the importance of the long tradition of *bel canto* – which had hitherto obtained in instrumental as well as in vocal music – but added to the semantic significance of orchestral sonorities.

Wagner's vocal lines (once thought to be unsingable), often angular and in themselves incomplete, are the source from which *Sprechstimme* (the kind of incantation mid-way between speech and song available in a whole range of works from Schoenberg to Maxwell Davies) derived. By the demonstrative use of *Leitmotivs* (a principle obtained from the *idée fixé* of Berlioz) Wagner aimed at dramatic credibility. Whether the recurrence of *Leitmotivs* – which are conveniently labelled in every relevant programme note – does in fact aid understanding is open to doubt. The principle, convenient as a structural device, is in any case, as worked by Wagner and Liszt, and, for that matter, Elgar is by now somewhat too naïve. Nonetheless the *Leitmotiv*, not being intended for development in the classical sense, went in the direction of the fragmentation of music, towards an appreciation of the sounds of music as sounds. The classic example of disintegration is, of course, the Prelude to *Tristan und Isolde*, in the opening of which the established principle that harmonies should move towards a predestined terminus was dislocated by the fact that here they seemed to go nowhere. The fact that they are inconclusive arose from the programmatic interpretation of the gloomy myth of the love of Tristan and Isolde. In one way and another Wagner up-graded the philosophic status of music. Music-drama became (what it had been in ancient times) a substitute for religious experience. It showed the possible function of music in revealing mythic values, in releasing forces that lie in the unconscious, and in restoring a belief in the virtues of magic. All of this is summarised in the position occupied by Wagner in the social history of Germany, and in the general sphere of musical experience.

In the 1870s the music of Wagner exercised a profound influence in France; more especially on the symbolist poets, Verlaine, and Mallarmé, but also on a somewhat disorderly music student, Claude Debussy. Somewhere this side of idolatry Debussy admired Wagner but felt that the methods of the composer would be improved if subjected to a course of Gallic refinement. Debussy also understood that European music need no longer be a closed shop. Harking back to the medieval (in general terms), having heard music by di Lasso and Palestrina in Rome, to the simpler sonorities and lucidity of the Renaissance polyphonists, and, by way of the folk-music played by various national groups at the International Exhibition in Paris in 1889, to the unfamiliar fascination of Far Eastern instrumentation. One feature of modern music is an absorbing interest in timbre, in tone-colour, in varied means of tone-production; in short in sound as an experience. This feature, of course, is there at the start, but Romanticism gave a new impetus to its exploitation. This was not always welcomed. When the

Viennese critic, Hanslick, heard Liszt's First Piano Concerto for the first time he went so far in the direction of above as to refer to it as the "Triangle Concerto". Though, as the listener may discover, it is not the introduction of the inoffensive triangle (and charming it is) that distinguishes this work, but the plasticity of the whole work.

An eclectic composer, whose formal structures grew from the nature of the musical purpose of the individual work, Debussy (who, as a student in Rome, met Liszt and drew inspiration from his keyboard inventiveness) indicated that no musical experiences were irrelevant to the central stream of the European tradition. By reducing the formalities of music and by concentrating attention on tone values – through negation of the rhetorical commonplaces of nineteenth century convention, and refinement of textures and dynamics – Debussy introduced Impressionist attributes. These, inspired in part by contemporary painters and also poets, were not derived from painting but from musical sources.

The quintessence of Debussy lives in *Pelléas and Mélisande*, conceivably the most moving operatic music of the twentieth century, but the easy way into the Debussy repertoire is by way of the two orchestral suites, *Nocturnes* and *La Mer*.

Nocturnes (night-pieces were a speciality of James McNeill Whistler, who was also living in Paris) comprises – "Nuages", an impression of the "changeless aspect of the sky and the slow solemn movement of the clouds, fading away in grey tones, lightly touched with white". This, in this sense, is colourless, but, in another, full of colour. Its subtleties stand out in comparison with the evocative application of heightened colour in the succeeding "Fêtes". The end-piece, "Sirènes", is a mystery, in which the sirens are represented by the voice-sounds of a wordless chorus of women's voices – with which may be compared the disembodied soprano voice – also without words – introduced by Vaughan Williams into the *Sinfonia Antartica*.

A good deal of this is archetypal. The clouds are, and the sea is. Unlike the Romantics Debussy, who in any case was an amoralist, does not moralise. In similar manner the three symphonic sketches of *La Mer* eliminate commentary and go as near to being what they are taken to represent as music can; always remembering that what is said to exist exists only in the mind of the observer. This goes back, somewhat, to Beethoven's intention (though Debussy said that he detested Beethoven's music) to give impressions of, rather than illustrations of, the countryside.

Wagner orchestrated in the grand manner, Debussy with delicacy and discretion, and his method comes out, comparatively speaking, as *pointillist*. From such reticence and such concentration on the single colour as is illustrated in Debussy's principal works sprang many of the techniques that are practised today.

Although it may appear otherwise, when historians and scholars have done their work of careful categorisation, the course which music pursues is affected by contingencies which could hardly have been predicted. The transmogrified romanticism of Schoenberg and his disciples (which later turned into a new orthodoxy) was helped along by the fact that it was born and bred under the interdict of political theorists. The fact that large numbers of artists, writers, and composers, from various countries in Eastern Europe flocked to Paris during the last years of the nineteenth and the first decade of the twentieth centuries was due also to political pressures. At the same time of course, Paris would have been a less desirable retreat had it not been for the general ferment of intellectual and aesthetic thought. So far as musicians were concerned Debussy occupied a focal position. This position was (unwillingly, on personal grounds) supported by Maurice Ravel.

Debussy's music, as also that of Ravel, was incentive to those who sought an escape from the Teutonic influences that had for more than a hundred years enwrapped the main part of European musical tradition. It was thus that in some cases a link between nationalism and impressionism was forged, while in others the vaguer aspirations of romantic nationalism were corrected by the application of the cooler critical standards of French musical method.

It is arguable that the greatest master of the twentieth century (so far as it has gone) is Igor Stravinsky. Apart from considerations of ranking Stravinsky is, without doubt, the most interesting composer of the age, not least because he is the most comprehensive. In a sense if one wished to study the whole music of an epoch through the works of a single master one would choose Stravinsky as the chief exemplar of that of the present age. As was Beethoven to one era, so is Stravinsky to another: whether the music of the one era is intrinsically superior to that of the other is ineligible for discussion. It was once convenient to slice up Beethoven's *oeuvre* into three "periods": the same fate has befallen Stravinsky – a sure warrant for entry into the Valhalla of the classics. This division into "periods" is a sterile occupation, for it denies the essential uniqueness of every work by a great artist. Thus a great composer who produces a thousand works shows a thousand different faces, and explores a thousand different "periods" of his own consciousness. In the end a major artist by being acutely aware of time stands outside it. This is the case with Stravinsky.

The comprehensiveness of Stravinsky is reflected by the nationalist content and form of expression of his early, still vital, ballet music of *The Firebird;* by the assimilation of baroque traits in, for instance, the freely re-assembled pieces of *Pulcinella* or the "Dumbarton Oaks" concerto for chamber orchestra; by the reflection of classical idealism in the Symphonies of 1940 and 1945; by the acknowledgment of the contrary claims of a binding liturgy in the superb *Symphony of Psalms* and the Mass; and of the popular market in the long-ago *Ragtime* for eleven instruments; by the theories of serialism and, indeed, aleatoricism, in such late works as *Movements for Piano and Orchestra.*

The story of Stravinsky is a record of coming to terms with circumstances, both extra-musical and musical. In the widest terms this is symbolised by the two-fold exploration of the pagan and the theo-centred motives within human nature. This gives *The Rite of Spring* at one extreme and, say, the *Canticum sacrum, Threni*, and *The Flood* at the other. In the final group there is the synthesis of the pagan and the religious, reflected in the sequence of dances of which the last work consists.

Here we become aware of the importance of the dance (enhanced by the wider cult of ballet) in contemporary musical thought and feeling. In the nineteenth century musical appreciation was based largely on the transference of word-concepts to music, on the literary interpretation of musical phenomena, on the supposed pre-eminence of the vocal line and of harmony in four parts (as settled in the convention of parts for soprano, alto, tenor, and bass). The end of this dominance was heralded by the emphasis on folk-dance during the resurgence of nationalism in the nineteenth century, but not finally effected until the emotional distinctions between dance and song were once more realised. Dance precedes song, a fact which is as evident now as it ever was. The importance of *The Rite of Spring* is that the fundamentals of the dance instinct (a ritualisation of the darker impulses that stir the conflicts of the psyche) are there fully exposed. This, of course, is why there was uproar when this work was first performed in Paris in 1913. In upsetting the prejudices of the bourgeois sense of morality it was, at least potentially, destructive of the social order. Since then, of course, half a hundred social orders have been overturned and *The Rite of Spring* exists as a classic in its own right. The pleasure derived from listening to it, however, is not the pleasure that comes from hearing a fine display of orchestral (and conducting) virtuosity, but that which stems from the relief afforded by the cathartic principle. *The Rite of Spring* is one of those musical experiences with which one may readily identify oneself.

We have already referred to the dichotomy of modern music (in the broad sense), but we may now begin to see that the two forms – of "popular" and "serious" – still have a common factor: rhythm. The basis of popular music is almost naked rhythmic pulsation, which, incidentally, accounts for the compulsion of Ravel's *Bolero*. The uncovering of the rhythmic potential of music of the other sort – a long process which went through the various phases of romanticism and nationalism – is the dominant feature in all modern styles. This rhythmic potential is, of course, a complex of patterns. There is the kind of non-rhythm (in the sense that beats in the bar cease to signify) that occurs in

Debussy's *L'Après-midi d'un faune*, in Sibelius's *Swan of Tuonela*, in the last movement of Holst's *The Planets*, or, for that matter, in the same composer's Prelude to the *Hymn of Jesus*. In other words the non-rhythm (to be appreciated in earlier music, as in the opening of Mendelssohn's *Midsummer Night's Dream* Overture) is programmatic. At the present time, in what is called *avante garde*, non-rhythm is present for no programmatic reason, but solely as a means of registering protest.

The opposite of non-rhythm is the kind of nervous patterning (also anti-beats-in-a-bar) of *The Rite of Spring*. At one time one rarely ventured beyond 5-beats-in-a-bar – agreeably and flexibly used by Tchaikovsky in the second movement of the *Symphonie Pathétique* and, with a purposive brashness, by Mussorgsky in the Promenade of *Pictures at an Exhibition*, but the collapse of what might be called accountant's symmetry (x beats in every bar, 4 or 8 bars in every phrase, and so on) has encouraged investigation of all manner of metrical dispositions.

In its human context (without which music does not effectively exist) musical style is the consequence of general attitudes. Underlying music are the unchangeable emotional relationships which are the substance of living. But above this emotional underlay is a variety of points of view, of mores. These are disposed in two main categories, the one of constructive, or conservative, the other of destructive, or revolutionary, character. We are, in the narrower terminology, back with the standing definitions of classical and romantic. The climate of the post-Romantic, era is, in every field, critical – to say the least. Thus it is that the virtues of normality are often shown as vices, and traits of abnormality as strength. The search for a new stability proceeds by way of revision of old conventions and by a process of disestablishment. In this context disestablishment in the first place meant the rejection of the claims of theorists and of dominant "schools". Thus the importance of the nationalists on the one hand, and of the non-nationalist Debussy on the other, in the twentieth century revolution.

The critical factor in music (exemplified in more extreme form by Erik Satie, from whom Debussy derived ideas at least) led to a diminution in the significance of melody and to an insistence on the primacy, in instrumental music, of rhythm. The importance of rhythm as such was emphasised, symphonically, by William Walton, whose First Symphony (heard complete for the first time in 1935), is one of the key works in the English symphonic tradition. In this work Walton raised the rhythmic inventiveness of the Overture *Portsmouth Point* (1925) – which, like a number of works of that period showed an awareness of the rhythmic vitality of jazz – to a higher degree. In his Symphony (as also in the oratorio *Belshazzar's Feast*) Walton enhanced the effect of sharp-edged rhythmic shocks by an astringency of harmony that at least demonstrates the fact that harmony (so-called) is not to be thought of as a self-sufficient entity, but as an amplification of movement – of parts and of sonorities. Apart from the works named Walton's popularity rests on the music for *Façade*, pieces originally contrived for small ensemble and as background to poems by Edith Sitwell, which is now generally known in the two orchestral suites. Wry, satirical, parodistic, these pieces serve to illuminate an important side of modern musical thought. A propensity to musical satire is, perhaps, particularly French – and the comedy of Saint-Saëns's *Carnival of Animals* – is in this sense a landmark.

Saint-Saëns, a prolific and probably under-rated composer, composed the *Carnival of Animals*, "a zoological fantasy", in 1886, and its relevance to later developments is indicated by its way-out instrumentation (piano and small instrumental group, including xylophone), by its economy of statement, and by its transmogrification of animal to human, or human to animal, properties. The *Carnival of Animals* is now amusing; but once it appeared grotesque.

Pleasure in the grotesque is, of course, not new. Its revival, however, has a special significance in relation to musical expression, and it may be noted that this links modern musical feeling to the temper of the Middle Ages just as effectively as conscious re-working of medieval compositional techniques. If one cares to, one may discover grotesque qualities in almost any representative modern work (depending on one's interpretation of the term). In an engaging form the grotesque is well delineated in such a work as Mussorgsky's *Pictures at an Exhibition*. The musical illustrations of the "Gnomes", of the Polish Jews "Samuel Goldenberg and Schmuyle", of the skulls in the Catacombs, of "The Hut on Fowls' Legs", belong to the province of music horror-literature – horror-comics maybe – and exert their fascination by the skilful provision of the unexpected contrast or gesture. This work is now normally heard in the orchestrated version of Ravel, but the pianist is advised to add the original version for piano, to his collection.

Musical experience is a mass of paradoxes. Exposition of the grotesque, and pleasure in malformation (of melodic or rhythmic contour, or instrumentation) is the obverse of the abiding desire to emulate Parsifal, and to attain some final absolution and purification. In the broad sense the revolutionary impulses in music during the last half-century were attempts to establish the truth. The business of returning to fundamentals was part of the process of seeking out musical purity. It may well be that this is no more than a chimera, but the search goes on. As has been shown on p. 84 child psychology, so to speak, has established itself as a factor in modern musical thought. Many composers are tumbling over themselves either to interpret the quality of childhood, or to provide musical material for the young that is not merely a hash-up of what goes for adults. On the whole those who succeed are those who avoid pretentiousness. Prokofiev's *Peter and the Wolf* (op. 67), for speaker and orchestra, is, like Saint-Saëns's *Carnival of Animals*, a "zoological phantasy" (he called it a "symphonic fairy-story for children") but amiable, materialistic, and eager. The insouciance of the work (composed for the new Central Children's Theatre in Moscow in 1936) disguises its structural efficiency. Looking beyond the narrative features of the music, based on well-defined *Leitmotivs*, one sees a three-part pattern of exposition, development (to the fight with the wolf), and recapitulation (in the form of a triumphal march).

"Modern music", then, is what you care to make of it.

8

Chamber Music

THE terms of reference which lie behind this book – that is, that it is for the possessor of a catholic selection of recordings – prompt the conclusion that for the reader for whom it is primarily intended all music is chamber music. Chamber music indicating, of course, music that is primarily for domestic, or, at least, private consumption. Musicologists spend much of their energy in urging authenticity of performance. They are, however, reluctant to make suggestions concerning authenticity of atmosphere. Yet to attain something to be thought near to the former without recreating something of the latter is hardly even half-way to the ideal. It can never be said too often that an audience is a necessary co-partner in the bringing to life of music (as also of drama). What music means is what the listener determines that it means.

So far as chamber music is concerned, the listener whose inclination to doubt his own competence is frequently strengthened by dogmas of criticism of one sort or another tends to react nervously. Chamber music, he believes, is the very height of musical rarefaction; composers set in immortality make a bee-line for (mainly) the string quartet – the medium above all mediums dedicated to the exploration of the absolute – and a handful of works which out-top all others in the same category serve to remind us of the ultimate mystique of musical expression.

There is some truth in this – as the works of Haydn, Mozart, Beethoven, Schubert, Brahms, and Bartók (to take the most obvious cases) testify – but it is often presented in a discouraging manner. The way in which quasi-religious values were transferred to aesthetics during the Romantic era has been responsible for the growth of a particularly reverential attitude towards chamber music in particular. That this form of music by its very nature is more "pure" and more "intellectual" than any other has no foundation in reason; only in a kind of aesthetic puritanism that is anyway to be deplored as a negation of the principles that underlie secular musical culture in western civilisation. Chamber music started out as entertainment. It became ritualised when affected by the formalities of the public concert. In the so-called golden age of chamber music, however, the special virtues later to be attached to such music were not yet recognised.

In 1790 the Princess Nicholas of Esterház died. "The prince is so overwhelmed . . .", wrote Haydn to Marianne von Genzinger, "that we had to strain every nerve to charm His Highness out of his sadness. I arranged a big programme of chamber music for the first three evenings . . . but the poor Prince fell into such profound melancholy on hearing my favourite Adagio in D that I had my work cut out to chase it away again with other pieces."

The conventional historian of music makes a genuflection at the name of Haydn, as that of the "Father of the String Quartet", and this has had the effect, across the years, of isolating the string quartet. What matters is not the medium, but the music. The province of chamber music is best explored by making a judicious selection from, as it is now said "across the board". From solo keyboard pieces, by way of duos, trios, quartets, and so on, to octets (e.g. Mendelssohn's Octet for strings in E flat, Op. 20), nonets (e.g. Spohr's "Grand" Nonet for violin, viola, cello, double-bass, flute, oboe, clarinet, horn, and bassoon in F major, Op. 21), and chamber orchestra (e.g. Mozart's *Eine kleine Nachtmusik*, or Wagner's *Siegfried Idyll*). Not, by the way, forgetting chamber music for voices, with or without instruments. On the lowest level of enjoyment such selection leaves the listener with a splendid opportunity of acquiring a taste for the finer flavours of musical tone.

This brings us to a point that has been so far given oblique and not quite serious reference. The composer of chamber music is working within a relatively limited field. With, say, one violin and one piano or even with four tonally compatible string instruments the appeal to the listener is less by way of striking contrasts of colour than by subtle tonal variations and by manipulation of the musical argument. Thus the design of chamber music often assumes a larger significance for the listener than the design of a work for an extensive orchestra. Maybe it should not; but it does. It is this fact that sometimes leads to negative criticism of certain works. Such as, for instance, Ravel's *Introduction and Allegro* for harp, string quartet, flute, and clarinet, which is less a logical pattern of thematic statements than an inspired sequence of delicate tonal tints, prompted in the first place by the personality of the harp.

In the first place, the present dichotomy between orchestral music and chamber music did not exist. If we pick up in the baroque era the concertos of Corelli were, for the most part, as much chamber music as his sonatas for one or two violins (with continuo). At the same period, moreover, vocal chamber music enjoyed at least equal status with instrumental. Alessandro Scarlatti poured out chamber cantatas as prolifically as Vivaldi turned out concertos. Such a cantata comprised a sequence of recitatives and arias, was for solo voice (sometimes more than one voice) with accompaniment either for continuo alone, or for a small group of instruments with continuo support.

The Scarlatti cantata (of which the pattern was cheerfully adopted by Handel, who left a large number of works of this order) was as significant in the early part of the eighteenth century as was the string quartet in the last part of the century. It was, in fact, the dominant form of *musica di camera*, ideal to room and to audience, and regulated to the requirements of both. Like the contemporary instrumental sonata the cantata was available for performance either by professional or amateur musicians. In chamber music, in general, it may be observed that until the twentieth century the dividing line between amateurs and professionals was less marked than in the larger forms of music. This does not, of course, mean that all chamber music was intended for amateurs to play; but some of it was, and that that was not was often designed for the pleasure of those who had some fairly intimate and practical acquaintance with music. The clubbable properties which belonged to the early days at least of the symphony obtained rather longer in respect of chamber music; which is an additional reason for the lingering notion that, being conceived for the *cognoscenti*, it was on a somewhat higher plane than some other forms of music.

As has already been suggested, since, today, virtually the whole of music can be confined to the home, all music has become a form of chamber music. Now the wish to reduce the broad experience of music to domestic properties is not a new one. In fact the solo cantata was opera brought down in scale. As we look around the field of domestic music in general in the earlier periods we discover a greater variety of similar reduction. Keyboard music of the sixteenth and seventeenth centuries represented arrangements of songs, dances, and secular and sacred part-songs, while the music of the same period for instrumental ensembles (or consorts, as they were frequently called) leaned heavily on idioms taken over from part-song and dance.

Throughout its modern, i.e. post Renaissance, history chamber music has kept an open window on the wider, public, world of music. The repertoire of the keyboard instruments, of course, is the best evidence of this. Thus the harpsichord suites of Handel often reflect the character of the opera (or oratorio) overture, just as the piano sonatas of Beethoven, although composed for the keyboard with a high degree of inventiveness, in one sense belong to the world of the symphony. There is, however, this difference. The keyboard works of Bach and Handel were intended for private pleasure; those of Beethoven, while serving private requirements, were eager to go out into the wider world. Hence the spacious character of the longer, and more rhetorical, piano sonatas. The "Pathétique", "Moonlight", and "Appassionata" Sonatas (of these sub-titles only the first was given by Beethoven) require a kind of public delivery that would destroy, for instance, the suites of Couperin, Bach, and Handel, and even many of the early classical sonatas.

It is, of course, difficult to realise that for the greater part of modern European history the majority of people knew only dimly, and at second or third hand, what was going on in the world. Domestic music, a universal means of communication, was one medium by which certain aspects of social, emotional, and intellectual, isolation were overcome. In the seventeenth and eighteenth centuries, at least, the music with which the music-lover was most intimately involved had a higher apparent content of reality than the same music – or, for that matter, much of the music of our own age – seems to present at this stage. For instance, the French models which J. S. Bach followed in respect of certain keyboard works, as well as the chamber-orchestral suites were not chosen solely on account of their aesthetic properties, but because it was official court policy (and Bach was a Court musician for a large part of his life) to inculcate a French style into the pattern of upper-class culture in the German States of the eighteenth century. The French-ness of Bach, therefore, meant one thing then, and another now.

For obvious reasons, chamber music was developed in (out-wardly) polite and well-to-do society. Its aristocratic origins have, perhaps, contributed something to the insecurity of chamber music in popular esteem (though the same kind of reservations have never obtained in the case of horse-racing). But there was not one, inflexible, aristocratic, mould. Each member of the aristocracy during the era of large-scale musical patronage, was an individual who, no matter how much he tried to conform to the ideal pattern, had individual tastes and opinions. Were it not so, the immense variety of classical music would have been impossible.

Throughout the eighteenth century the illusion that the age could be regarded as the Age of Reason was widely held. The intelligent pursued the cult of rationalism, and, as it happens, chamber music became an ideal medium for idealisation of the cult. Here we arrive at the finally accepted special status of the string quartet, a finely balanced medium in which dialectical problems of a musical nature could be adequately, but calmly, discussed. As has been suggested such discussion kept in mind what was under observation elsewhere.

Now the intimacy of the medium is often a particular

attraction to the composer, enabling him sometimes to be more personal than when exercising a more public, and spectacular function. This is why in the introduction to his so-called "Dissonance" Quartet Mozart reveals ideas not otherwise exposed by him; why Beethoven's last quartets lie outside the limits of late Classical propriety; why Debussy's last sonatas are, even for him, speculative; why Schoenberg and Webern virtually scorned all combinations other than those which, in the broad sense, were of the chamber music class. In the last case, however, it should be observed that the older significance of chamber music as social music had all but disappeared.

It is by now, no doubt, obvious that music so far from being regulated by the set points laid out in theory is in a continual state of flux, with ever-changing relationships between composers and performers, and between both and their audiences.

The norm of baroque chamber music was the trio sonata (or the suite), for 2 violins (or flutes), cello and harpsichord. This constitution satisfied the requirements of the averagely musical household, whether the participating players were amateur or professional. (It was only establishments maintained on a princely scale that went in for larger instrumental groups – and even then such groups were more modest than is sometimes thought.) It also satisfied the ambitions of composers for whom clarity of outline and brilliance of sonority were the principal objectives. The obvious lacuna in the ensemble is the viola. The truth was that the viola was not taken very seriously, and even in orchestral works its role was limited. In symphonic music it continued to do little more than double the bass line until well into the second part of the eighteenth century. The truth was that since the middle sonorities were supplied by the harpsichord and since this fact enhanced the brightness of the upper parts and left the line of the bass unimpeded the arrangement was perfectly satisfactory.

Change often takes place within an art fortuitously. Two factors combined to alter the chamber music norm. One was the impracticability of using a keyboard instrument out of doors; the other was the gradual extinction of the harpsichord by the pianoforte – an instrument from the start that was designed to

CHAMBER

Members of the Melos Ensemble (l. to r. Emanuel Hurwitz (violin), Neill Sanders (horn), Gervase de Peyer (clarinet), William Waterhouse (bassoon), Cecil Aronowitz (viola), Terence Weil (cello), John Gray (double bass) recording.

ORCHESTRAL

Daniel Barenboim conducting a Mozart symphony with the English Chamber Orchestra, whose numbers approximate to an orchestra of the composer's time. The location is No. 1 Studio, Abbey Road and the recording producer in attendance is Suvi Raj Grubb.

BALLET
Margot Fonteyn and Rudolf Nureyev in a scene from Tchaikovsky's "Swan Lake" (photo from the Unitel film featuring these artists).

OPERA
The interior of the Rome Opera House where many important operatic recordings have been made.

SACRED MUSIC
King's College Choir under their conductor David Willcocks recording in the famous Chapel at Cambridge.

BAROQUE
Venice was one of the most important centres of Baroque music, and this illustration of Bellini's Procession in the Piazza San Marco was an ideal occasion for the performance of some of the great works by such composers as Monteverdi and Andrea and Giovanni Gabrieli.

CONCERTO

Yehudi Menuhin is here recording the Beethoven Violin Concerto with Otto Klemperer conducting the New Philharmonia Orchestra in the Kingsway Hall, London.

CHORAL — ORCHESTRAL

Sir John Barbirolli is seen conducting a recording of Elgar's "Dream of Gerontius" in the Free Trade Hall, Manchester. Richard Strauss recognised the work as a masterpiece which led to its establishment in the choral repertoire.

fulfil a more independent role than the harpsichord. The piano-forte arrived at a time when the emotional properties of music were being more extensively exploited. At the same time the colour potential of the viola also came to be recognised.

The great composers (at any rate until the twentieth century) have become such, not despite but on account of their pro-lificacy. The opportunities open to a composer in the eighteenth century (even if usually materially unrewarding) enabled him to explore practically every current musical form. Out of such explorations new forms arose. As a young man Josef Haydn wrote string trios (which assumed keyboard support), diverti-menti (suites of pieces of no prescribed number) for various combinations of instruments, keyboard sonatas, and sym-phonies. Of the divertimenti some were playable by four stringed instruments. In fact, if they were played out-of-doors, it was convenient that they should be. The first dozen or so of what are now categorised as string quartets were in fact diverti-menti, or, when the number of movements was reduced to three or four, symphonies – as the term was then understood. By 1750, or thereabouts, Haydn attracted by the tonal possibilities and the flexibility of the combination, had settled the status of the string quartet. That he was able to do so was due to the creative freedom he enjoyed as musician to the Esterházy family, and to his close friendship with his instrumental col-leagues at Eisenstadt.

In half a century Haydn composed more than 80 string quartets, which in their own sphere are as significant as the church cantatas of Bach or the symphonies of Beethoven (not to mention the symphonies of Haydn himself). Their distinction is their universality – both of emotion and of technical ac-complishment. Regarding the latter one notes the facility of the part-writing, based on an absorption of north German con-trapuntal practice, and the extensiveness of thematic devolution across the formal structures of sonata form, minuet and trio (to which Haydn brought a new intensity), and air and varia-tions. Regarding the former the range is from the Magyar content of certain movements (e.g. the *allegretto alla Zingarese* of op. 20, no. 4), across the innocence of the "Lark" Quartet

(Op. 33 No. 3) and the dignities of the "Emperor" (Op. 76 No. 3), to the profound heart-searching of the *adagio* of Op. 77 no. 1.

In some ways the most human among the greatest composers Haydn is also perhaps the least appreciated. It is a curious fact, repertoire-wise he is, in general, indifferently represented. That this is so is partly because his life enclosed that of Mozart, partly because he stayed put in Eisenstadt, Esterház, and Vienna, until in old age he was able to explore further afield. There are those, however, who have suffered worse at the hands of posterity than Haydn; among them some whose reputation was almost as great as and who made much more of a success of life than, either Haydn or Mozart. These included Johann Christian Bach, Johann George Albrechtsberger, Carl Ditters von Dittersdorf, Luigi Boccherini, and Emanuel Aloys Förster. Apart from the first, the others, perhaps, are not even names, yet by reference to their activities (as also of a hundred other musicians of the same period) we realise how firmly the idea of what we now generically term "classical" chamber music took root. We also realise what variety there was within this field, and also to what extent composers were interdependent. In one way or another the composers named were part of the Haydn-Mozart-Beethoven complex that was the classical school.

J. C. Bach was a stylist, with a preference for the elegancies that he admired when, before coming to London, he was Cathedral organist in Milan. A good judge of middle-brow taste he composed chamber music that entices by reason of its cool beauty, and by the variety of its instrumentation. There is a direct line to Mozart, to whom J. C. Bach was an early hero, by way of the symphonies on the one hand and by such works as the Flute Quartet in F on the other. Albrechtsberger, a Viennese teacher and theorist, was famous for his skill in counterpoint which is reflected in his forty-four fugal quartets and which was put at Beethoven's disposal when, in 1794–5, he was a pupil of Albrechtsberger. The consequences of this teaching were profound – as witness the contrapuntal mastery of Beethoven's later works, particularly the "Hammerklavier Sonata" (Op. 106), and the Quartets in B flat (op. 130), and C

130

sharp minor (op. 131), and the "Grosse Fuge" (op. 133) originally intended as the finale of the Op. 130 Quartet.

Albrechtsberger was a friend of Haydn, as also was the amiable von Dittersdorf, whose capacity for gauging popular taste was symbolised by the bestowal of a Papal Knighthood (an honour also given to Gluck and to Mozart). An excellent violinist, von Dittersdorf was often able to make his music sound better than intrinsically it was. "He," it was said, "speaks to the heart." Haydn was glad not only of von Dittersdorf's companionship but also of his advice. There have been some famous string quartets, but one which we would most like to have heard consisted of Haydn (first violin), von Dittersdorf (second violin), Mozart, (viola), and Vanhall (cello). Stephen Storace, an English pupil of Mozart, noted how he once had heard this group in 1785 in Vienna.

Boccherini, a cellist (represented in the cellist's repertoire by four graceful concertos that bear a close relationship to the more forceful Cello Concerto by Haydn), imparted all the graces of Italy to chamber music. He is best known for his predilection for the string quintet – with two cellos, and was as popular in France, Spain, and Germany, as he was in Italy. Although they never met there was a mutual respect between him and Haydn, while Mozart's earliest string quartets were inspired by those of Sammartini and Boccherini that he encountered during his early Italian visits. In contrast to Boccherini when writing quintets Mozart preferred two violas to the two cellos.

Emanuel Förster was another Viennese musician – at whose house chamber music parties attended by the best players in Vienna took place twice a week. Förster himself composed some 48 string quartets, the importance of which lies in the fact that they (or some of them) persuaded Beethoven to take lessons from Förster. The value of these lessons was particularly in respect of the techniques of composition for string quartet he generously acknowledged.

It becomes apparent that what is now regarded as the regular classical chamber music repertoire is but a very small part of a vast body of works of differing quality, character, and intention. Of those whom we tend rudely to call "minor composers" some

131

composed chamber music for the general amateur market – then rapidly extending. It may here be observed that this market also imposed its own – at least para-classical – standards; of clarity, economy, and logic. Formalism, or formality, had more than one origin. Other composers, Förster, for instance, appear to have considered their own interests and those of their colleagues. Still others were concerned with the requirements of patrons who wanted to listen rather than to perform; what is more, to listen to music which seemed to reflect, in an ideal form, the qualities that they presumed themselves to possess.

Necessarily, we (unless practising chamber musicians) come into this world from the outside. In so doing, and lacking the advantages of those to whom "chamber music" was no rarity and for whom commentaries on it were neither thinkable nor necessary, we tinge appreciation with reverence. So we may read, in a recent notice of a Mozart performance: " . . . The three great string quintets in C, G minor, and D . . . above all the C major, have a good claim not only to be regarded as Mozart's supreme masterpieces but to represent the art of music in its highest form." I find this kind of adulation merely irritating, since it is quite without meaning. It is also liable to upset the digestive processes of the keen listener.

Nonetheless, we must accept the primacy of the chamber music of Haydn and Mozart in the latter part of the eighteenth century because of a high degree of invention, a superb technical accomplishment, and that synoptic quality that marks out the greater artist from the lesser. Some composers (von Dittersdorf, for instance) appreciated certain aspects of musical expression which they exploited with a good deal of success. Haydn and Mozart, however, understood, it seems, the whole range of possibilities.

The synoptic quality of classical music is nowhere better suggested than in the six string quartets published by Mozart in the autumn of 1785, and dedicated to Haydn. During the time he was busy on these quartets (their composition was spread over two or three years) Mozart was feverishly active in many directions. In 1784–5 at least seven piano concertos – including the masterpieces in D minor (K.466), E flat (K.482), and C major (K.467) – were produced; as well as a large amount of varied chamber music; including the Quintet in C minor for piano and wind instruments (K.452), and the Piano Quartet in G minor (K.478), while a start was made on *The Marriage of Figaro*, and the oratorio, *Davidde penitente*, was constructed from the music of the unfinished Mass in C minor. The commitment of the composer to so many projects meant that none could be independent of the others. This was also a year of intimacy with Haydn, during which the older master made his much quoted observation to Leopold Mozart (Wolfgang's father) to the effect that Wolfgang was the greatest composer of his acquaintance.

As has already been stated Mozart was in the habit, during 1785, of taking part with Haydn and others in the private performance of chamber music. The experience, and gratitude to Haydn, prompted him, therefore, to issue a new set of quartets – the first that he had composed for almost a decade. It should be remembered that as further incentive to this form of composition was the issue of Haydn's Opus 33 Quartets in 1781, in the Preface to which Haydn drew attention to their "new and special manner".

In the first of his Opus X series (K.387) Mozart alluded to the gaiety of Haydn in the opening movement, and paid tribute to his fugal mastery in the concluding movement. Otherwise it is to be noticed to what extent the instruments had become emancipated – and in particular the viola, and how Mozart was expanding the emotional resources both of the medium and of music in general. The three factors contributing most to this expansion are the evocative contours of melodic outline (as in the stormy trio in G minor and the far-distant, and ethereal, *Andante cantabile*); the subtlety and variety accorded to the texture by the exploitation of chromatic inflection both of melody and harmony; and the siting of dynamics.

Mozart's contemporaries often discovered in his music a new kind of melancholy, that was both perplexing and captivating. The assumption of a gentle melancholia was part of the expected behaviour of a music-lover in the Age of Reason. Mozart stripped away the pretence, and showed the truth – that melancholy, malaise, discontent, were endemic in human nature. The thesis that Mozart's chamber music is "abstract" is destroyed at every turn. Consider, for instance, the chromatic motiv at the beginning of the Minuet of the G major Quartet, in which the sounds alternate between soft and loud, *piano* and *forte*. Most of all, of course, there is the famous opening of the "Dissonance" Quartet (K.465), which, within the terms of Mozart's style, has the tension of Bach. This is an adventure into the realm of the unknown – the mysteries that lay about *The Magic Flute* as explored without the necessity to consider a specific theatrical tradition. And yet, the classical composer held fast to his belief in the eventual victory of reasonableness. After the *Adagio* of the C major Quartet Mozart proceeds to demonstrate all the virtues of clear argument evolved from within earshot of the courtesies of the *galant* style.

The minor composer may very well be as much a master, of an idiom, or a style, as a greater one. The quality of charm that belongs to the so-called *galant* manner may be appreciated in hundreds of symphonies, quartets, quintets, and so on, by contemporaries of Haydn and Mozart. In many cases, however, it may be felt that there is a narcissistic character about such works – this character is, perhaps, even more evident in stylistically "perfect" poetry, or prose. Haydn, a formulator of stylistic principles, was, to some extent, free of the dangers inherent in the narrower forms of efficiency. Mozart, as precise a composer as any who lived, inherited formulas that could have encouraged a sense of self-sufficiency in the effective handling of these formulas. But Mozart looked outward from the structural centure of the music of his age, and in so doing proportioned each work according to the claims of human interest.

We owe the Clarinet Quintet (K.581) and the Clarinet Concerto (K.622) not only to Mozart, but also to the clarinettist for whom both works were composed. Mozart, in fact, referred to the former as "Stadler's Quintet".

Anton Stadler was a close friend of Mozart during the last ten years of Mozart's life. He was also, like Mozart, a member of the fraternity of Viennese Freemasons – with which cult, through the music of *The Magic Flute*, the clarinet may be said to be associated. Both the Quintet and the Concerto, revealing the many-sided character of the tone of the instrument and testing the virtuosity even of a modern player (see the final set of Variations) show the extent to which the composer had studied the instrument as used by a masterly performer. In the Quintet the solo instrument certainly takes the lead; but its function is enhanced by the fact that the stringed instruments, by their observations and commentary, give it due encouragement. This is clear from the outset, where the scene is laid by the strings, and into which the clarinet inserts itself only when it has, so to speak, become acclimatised.

During his lifetime Mozart, as a man, was execrated by some and despised by others. After his death he was, of course, idealised. He was the great liberator of music, the harbinger of romantic thought, as well as the arbiter of classical design. Just as in judging fugal music one turns back to the criterion provided by the works of Bach, so in respect of chamber music one returns to Mozart: probably, unconsciously, to the Mozart as idealised in the immediate post-classical period. Even then his music, invested with the aura and authority that accumulates about works that have survived from a previous generation, suggested a golden age that had forever gone.

After an evening of chamber music in the summer of 1816 Franz Schubert wrote in his diary that Mozart "in the darkness of our life shows us a far-off region, bright, clear, and beautiful, in which we may confidently hope." On February 6, 1826, Beethoven wrote to the Abbé Maximilian Stadler that he had "always been among those who had praised Mozart most highly, and so he would remain until his last breath!" Towards the end of the nineteenth century Brahms observed in a letter to Hans von Bülow: "Today we cannot any more write so beautifully as Mozart could: what we can do, however, is to see to it that we write as clearly as he did."

Schubert, Beethoven, Brahms, all Viennese musicians and, therefore, living within the Mozartian tradition, show their devotion to Mozart nowhere more clearly than in their chamber works.

The chamber music of Beethoven forms a special category of its own. Not only does it contain the essence, indeed the quintessence of Beethoven's musical thought, it also represents a point of division in musical practice. Up to the end of the eighteenth century chamber music, whatever its intrinsic quality, was, by intention and often by disposition, domestic. In theory, at least, the chamber works of Haydn and Mozart were practicable for amateurs. Those of Beethoven, on the whole, are not. The collaboration of professional and virtuoso players with composers has already been noted. From the time of Beethoven onwards the composer thought almost exclusively of interpretation through the highly skilled, and chamber music was invested with a new function. It became the medium for the composer's more profound observations, such as were to be appreciated by the initiated rather than the uninitiated. Chamber music performances necessarily attracted smaller audiences than orchestral music (because it was performed in smaller auditoriums), and thus a higher degree of concentration on the part of the listener was at least implied.

The place of the virtuoso in nineteenth century music is illustrated by the violin and piano, and cello and piano, sonatas of Beethoven. In respect of the former the composer had in mind the characteristics and special virtues of such players as George Bridgetower, the mulatto violinist from London, who, together with Beethoven, gave the first performance of the "Kreutzer" Sonata (op. 47) at a concert in Vienna in 1803, and Pierre Rode, the French virtuoso, and (like Kreutzer) pupil of Viotti, for whom the G major sonata (Op. 96) was composed. "I must," said Beethoven, in discussing this work, "take into consideration Rode's style of playing." The first two of Beethoven's cello sonatas (Op. 5, nos. 1 and 2) were composed in 1796 for Jean Pierre Duport, cellist to the King of Prussia (who was also an amateur cellist for whom Mozart had written his "Prussian Quartets"). The third of the Cello Sonatas, completed in 1808, is one of Beethoven's masterpieces of logical construction. Covering a wide compass it is also clearly a virtuoso piece. The fourth and fifth Sonatas, written for Joseph Linke, a member of the famous Viennese quartet led by Ignaz Schuppanzigh, appeared in 1815, as Opus 102. More introspective than the third sonata these are of considerable interest as showing Beethoven at grips with the problem of establishing convincing formal procedures for an unusual combination, and the finale of the last sonata is a demonstration of belief in the regenerative processes of fugal form. Regarding this Beethoven said that ". . . a new and really poetical element must be introduced into the traditional form."

The unity of a musical work is dependent on balance. That is what form is about. The achievement of a new sense of balance is most evident, of course, in the relationship in the violin and cello sonatas of string and keyboard instrument. The piano, as it was not in the previous era, is now established as a partner in the combination with an equal share-holding.

The development of the role of the piano by Beethoven – whether in conjunction with and opposition to the orchestra through the concerto medium, or within chamber music, or as an independent force in conveying the aspirations of a new age – was one of the most important factors in the expansion of music. The three characteristics of the piano that were initially important were its percussive quality, its dynamic range, and – perhaps most significant of all – its capacity for *cantabile*. All of these qualities are evident in what, by name at least, is, perhaps, Beethoven's most familiar work of chamber music – the "Archduke Trio", of which the opening of the slow movement, by piano alone, is among the most serene moments in the whole of music. The first public performance of the trio (inscribed to Beethoven's pupil and friend, the Archduke Rudolph) took place in 1814, Beethoven playing the piano, Schuppanzigh the violin, and Linke, the cello. The "Archduke" Trio held a special place in German music and in the later cult of Beethoven. When the Beethoven statue was unveiled in Bonn in 1845 the slow movement, with words from Goethe, was sung as a hymn. At the Centenary Celebrations of 1870 the same movement was performed in an orchestral version by Liszt.

The chamber music of Beethoven ranges from the conventional, sometimes utilitarian, works written in youth in Bonn to the late and unique string quartets. In an absolute sense this music (as indeed all of Beethoven's music) represents a spiritual pilgrimage: man in search of the ideal. In this the music takes on a philosophical quality, which, in the end, removes the music from the confines of time and leaves the listener beyond and over emotional responses and poised on the edge of answers to the unanswerable. If Beethoven among musicians is the hardest to understand then the most difficult of philosophers is Hegel – Beethoven's contemporary who was born in the same year, 1770. There is not space here to expound on Hegelian theses which may seem to be reflected in Beethoven's music, and it must suffice to say that Hegel's career was dedicated to giving intellectual credibility to mystical experience by means of proof of the supremacy and indissolubility of the Idea, or Reason, otherwise the True, the Eternal.

The fascination of Beethoven lies, partly at least, in appreciation of his capacity for intellecualising (i.e. formalising) mystical experiences, and the labour that this entailed is shown in the progress of works through various phases in the extant sketches.

Beethoven lived in Vienna, but he was a German, not least in the manner in which he promoted the philosopher's cause of music. In this respect he may be seen as the descendant of Bach (of whose music he became aware through his first Bonn teacher, Christian Neefe, who was of the school of Leipzig). In Schubert, on the other hand, we see the greater spontaneity of the Austrian. Beethoven and Schubert were both immeasurably indebted to Mozart (a Salzburger of German stock, and not, in the ethnic sense, a true Austrian), but each was influenced by different aspects of that master's works. Schubert was inspired by the pure melodiousness of Mozart, by the clarity and fluency of his textures, and by the magical quality of his coloured harmonies. The genius of Schubert, however, lay in the immediacy of his perception – which created songs out of the imagery evoked by single words, and symphonies out of tunes. In the field of chamber music, the synthesis of Schubert's visions is achieved in the "Trout" Quintet, a work of large scale to be set beside the "Great" C major Symphony, the Quintet in C (with two cellos) and the *Fantasy* (Op. 15) for piano. The relationship between the latter work and the Quintet is established by the inclusion in each of a set of variations on a song, on "The Wanderer" in the one, and "The Trout" in the other. Unusually, for he was not greatly interested in virtuosity for its own sake, "The Wanderer" is a virtuoso type of work; so too is the Quintet, but in a different way. Here the virtuosity consists of the exposition of the tonal properties of the participating instruments, and in the extension of ideas which are lyrical into a dramatic framework. "Certain works of Schubert," wrote the French critic L.-A. Bourgault-Ducoudray, "resemble tropical forests, with all the variegation of butterfly-wings, the dream-like colouring of the birds, with unknown scents, and unsuspected efflorescences . . ." The "Trout" Quintet, with its exuberant sense of joy in living, belongs to this category. Schubert, perhaps, is not generally thought of as a pioneer of "modern music" – in the sense that Beethoven is – but it is worth noting that the French critic of forty years ago picked up from Schubert a feeling of luxuriance that (with more direct tropical inspiration) may be appreciated in the larger works of Messiaen.

Music is seen as the result of the fusion of ideas, of styles, of personal interests, and so on, that are not at first sight always to be seen as compatible. Fusions of this nature are, of course, part of the process of development; but by sticking too closely to a merchanistic conception of development there is a danger of getting the arithmetic of appreciation wrong. Brahms lived in Vienna (so did a lot of musicians who have been forgotten) and formed his musical ideas out of a due consideration of the classical proprieties. Therefore he is ranked in the Mozart–Beethoven group, as a "classical" composer, and in danger of acceptance by the unwary as a kind of composite figure. Part of the difficulty of getting to know Brahms (here one speaks in general, and not in particular) is that, in a popular sense, he had no biography. That is to say, his biography makes unglamorous reading. For myself I like Tchaikovsky's picture – of "a little man with a great paunch, who drank too much." This, not least, is a corrective to the frequent picture of an inhibited recluse, ill at ease in society, and even more ill at ease with women. Brahms was one of the great European composers, who accepting the disciplines of the baroque-classical tradition brought that tradition through the channels of Romanticism and, seemingly to an end.

More than any other nineteenth century composer Brahms, perhaps, made music a vehicle for the expression of the deepest personal feelings – those feelings that escape the definition of words. In no works are the patterns of personal feeling more evident than in the chamber works, which ranging from the B major Piano Trio (Op. 8) of 1854, with echoes of Beethoven's *Ode to Joy* in the opening theme, to the Clarinet Quintet in B minor (Op. 115) of 1891 cover a period of forty years.

One of the most powerful influences on Brahms was his friendship with the Schumanns. Between the introspections of Schumann's music and those of Brahms's there are obvious similarities, but, more disciplined by temperament and by Clara Schumann with whom he was probably in love, Brahms leaves no suggestion of morbidity. On the other hand his compensatory exuberances are less unbridled. Thus, in an age which was becoming increasingly concerned with the superficial aspects of music, Brahms proclaimed the virtues of the classical and stoical temper.

Brahms was one who aimed at avoiding what he considered to be inessentials, and some of his most pregnant works are those in which he deliberately limits his options. One notes the relative absence of rhetoric from the Piano Concertos, the austere foundation of the finale of the Fourth Symphony, the elimination of violin from the second of the two orchestral Serenades (both of which may be considered virtually as chamber music), the terseness of the C minor Piano Quartet, and the austerity of the Organ Preludes. In all of these, however, there are moments of tenderness that cancel any sense of lack of sympathy. In the general repertoire of chamber music Brahms's two Sextets (2 violins, 2 violas, 2 cellos) – the first in B flat major (Op. 38), of 1859/60, the second in G major (Op. 36), composed some five years later, are the first familiar works for such a combination. This particular combination no doubt commended itself to Brahms on account of the warmth of the texture.

In the first – a kind of relief for the composer after the turbulances of the D minor Piano Concerto – the open-air lyricism akin to that of Schubert is given full rein. This indeed, is one of the most engaging of Brahms's works, and it gained immediate popularity in Germany. The second Sextet, less colourful than the first, and regarded as "obscure" when first heard, is more subtle, more contrapuntal, and – it may seem – more deeply felt. Like Beethoven, Brahms was a great master of the slow movement, in that he could achieve a state of beneficent calm without losing mobility. The slow movements of both Sextets are sets of variations. The initial utterance of that of the second Sextet is one of Brahms's most profound musical utterances and carries the high seriousness of Bach in its complex of melody, counterpoint, and chromatic harmony. The conclusion of the Clarinet Quintet, composed for the clarinettist Richard Mühlfeld of Meiningen, is also in variation form. This Quintet, like that of Mozart, is an embodiment of the personality of the clarinet – but the clarinet as it had come to be understood in Brahms's day. That is, the nearest equivalent in instrumental to vocal sonority. This matter of personalisation was the distinctive feature of Romanticism in music (and the basis of many of our reactions) and the Clarinet Quintet of Brahms is perhaps, the point of no return within Romantic territory. An elegiac, though also rhapsodic, work it is all of a piece, and its unity is emphasised by the repetition of the theme of the first movement in the last. The Clarinet Quintet was first performed at the Court of Meiningen – the last of the little German Courts, that had done so much for music, to survive. It is worth reflecting that Meiningen was raised to its musical eminence by Bach's cousin, Johann Ludwig, and that its tradition carried just beyond Brahms and Wagner (who drew Meiningen players into his Bayreuth orchestra) to catch up with Elgar, whose "*Enigma Variations*" were gratefully received into the repertoire of the ducal orchestra by Fritz Steinbach.

9

Music and Voice

DELIBERATELY, the last chapter left off with Brahms, with reference to whom this may well commence. For he was almost the last great composer in whose works the age-old unity of vocal and instrumental expression was retained. In crude terms, one may listen to the pianoforte, chamber, and orchestral works of Brahms and recognise "tunes". This tunefulness is backed by the fact that the composer was among the three or four most distinguished exponents of the German Lied – in itself a demonstration of the unity heretofore mentioned. Since Brahms's time attempts to re-assert the pristine unity of vocal-instrumental expression – as particularly by Kodály and Vaughan Williams – have been more than a little self-conscious (See the solitary symphony of the former, and the *Pastoral* and Fifth – offshoot of *The Pilgrim's Progress* – Symphonies of the latter), and even aggressive.

At the beginning of the twentieth century the mystique attached to vocal, particularly choral, music had been all but destroyed; now, however, largely through revival of master-pieces of the Renaissance and Baroque periods that had long been neglected, something of this mystique has returned. At least, the listener, suspending disbelief, is willing to be swept into a new experience of raptures with the polyphony of Palestrina, the *seconda prattica* of Monteverdi, the culminating Lutheranism of Bach, the coloured ritual of Catholicism as interpreted by Berlioz or Verdi, and so on. Choral music is playing a part in a counter-revolution – the counter-revolution that goes under various labels of which neo-Romanticism is the most convenient. At the same time the mood of neo-

Romanticism is removed from that which formerly obtained in respect of "sacred" music. In former times music of this order was (at heart, at least) propaganda – and highly effective it frequently was. So effective indeed that to the mostly non-committed contemporary mind various forms of religious music not only derive from particular creeds, but may be said to be those creeds. Taken together – and we are able to listen, comparatively, to Schütz and Victoria, to Handel and to Rossini, as exponents of religion-inspired music – what we listen to now forms a corpus of a humanist's faith – if this is not too extreme a paradox – in the supernal.

This is where we are. But we are where we are because of a process of change that set in perhaps a hundred years ago. There was then a partial collapse of the religious beliefs with which, it should be noted, the musical potential of the human voice was so intimately associated. At the same time the significance of the latter was diminished by the apparently limitless communicative powers of instruments. As has been seen the word-music nexus found a home in all forms of instrumental music, and the dominant forms of concert overture and symphonic poem were, so to speak, songs without words. The luxuriance of late Romanticism, however, produced a reaction towards austerity, and as soon as this took hold it was noted that the virtues of vocal, especially choral, music were greater than had been thought. When the techniques of Bach came back through renovated contrapuntal procedures there was a tacit acknowledgment of the values embedded in traditional choral polyphony. The Bachian strain was strong in Brahms, not only in particular but also in general terms. Brahms, born in Hamburg, was heir to a north German seriousness that was, indeed, the catalytic force in his expression.

The expressionism of Bach, however, was centred on doctrines that were less meaningful in the age of Brahms. He, a free-thinker, summarised his philosophy in a *German Requiem* that, liturgically, speaking, is no Requiem, in the *Alto Rhapsody*, and in the *Song of Destiny* (or "Fate"). The text of the first of these works was taken from Luther's translation of the Bible, and centred on the theme of mortality and the promise of immortality. The *Alto Rhapsody*, the words from Goethe's "Winter Journey in the Harz Mountains", is analogous to the *Requiem* in the general sense that it finds men as no more than a plaything of the fates, to be redeemed by the power of love. The poem of Friedrich Hölderlin which is the foundation of the *Song of Destiny* deals with very much the same sentiments. Behind these works stands the symbol of Faust and, to some extent, the severe Faustian music of Schumann.

Each of these works is symphonic to the extent of being constructed according to formal patterns – thematic development and sectional repetition (note the enclosing movements of the *Requiem* and the *Song of Destiny* that bring these works into a kind of circular unity by the fact of the end of each being the same as the beginning). There is also a strong independence of rhythmic pattern, most eloquently exposed in the funeral march – the second movement – of the *Requiem*, and most subtly in the pervasive triplet movement of the *Song of Destiny*. But these factors are felt not as independent and self-sufficient, but as an extension of the textural concepts. Such extension does not lead to exteriorising – that is ideas are not caught up into onomatopoeiac instrumental gestures (indeed, as in the violinless opening of the *Requiem*, the point is made that effectiveness derives more within this context from exclusion than from inclusion) and thus attention is drawn towards the meaning of the text. In his choral movements Brahms remembers the traditions of seventeenth century German cantata–motet style, (the setting of the word "blessed" in the *Requiem* is remarkably similar to that of Schütz in a funeral motet). So far as the solo voice is concerned – as in the fifth movement of the *Requiem* and in the meltingly beautiful alto part in the *Rhapsody* – the composer circles round from the solos to be found also in seventeenth century German cantata, by way of the warm simplicities of solo song in the native *Singspiel*, to the emotion-laden, harmonically charged, *Lied* of the nineteenth century, that was thus in direct line of decent from a long song tradition.

Music for the voice is affected by two factors that live without the sphere of music as such. The first is the condition of literature and its relevance at any particular point in time; the second is the institutions that accommodate and, to a large extent, control musical function. The development of techniques, out of which grow styles, may be seen by some as an inevitable consequence of the "progress" of music in general, but truthfully this should be regarded as ensuing from the often unconscious inclination to purposive acceptance of the disciplines implied by more general considerations.

The solo song of the seventeenth century, most splendidly demonstrated by John Dowland and Henry Purcell, was not only a response to the Italian preference for monody to polyphony but also to a desire to establish the independence and integrity of the individual. In both cases one is aware that the vocal line is inspired by feeling, that the song has been made a vehicle of personality, or individuality. This, as may be discovered from almost any interpretation, ties up with the place of the solo singer in the scheme of things. The solo artist, especially the solo singer whose individual gifts were unique was, in fact, a symbol. Solo song (the cantatas of Scarlatti and those who followed his example) was also a symbol of the domestication of music, of the reduction of issues to examination in relative privacy. The songs of Dowland and Purcell, as of Thomas Augustine Arne of the next generation, were also protestations of affection for the native language. In the sixteenth century an English composer happily set Latin texts, in the eighteenth century he no longer did so.

By the time English composers had come to terms with the indigenous literary tradition the Germans had no literary tradition, apart from Luther, with which they could come to terms. From the time of Luther, however, the determination to establish a German literature was strong. The medium for implementation of the intention was the "Academy" – the aristocratic, later bourgeois, intellectual club founded on similar lines to those that had previously flourished in Italy and France – whose members met together to promote culture in a society whose general philistinism was deplored. The German cultural *Gesellschaft* had a long and complicated history, with consequences in many fields, which may be seen from one point of view as being assembled round a hard core of musical endeavour.

The Germans were a very musical nation. That they were was due to the particular way in which singing (since Luther made it a point of policy to exploit the art) had become, much more than a branch of "art", a way of life. The solo song for private use, had an honoured place during the period of the Enlightenment in Germany, as is instanced by the few songs of J. S. Bach that have survived. Of these some, but not all, were of a broadly religious nature in so far as the words were concerned, but stylistically there was no division between sacred and secular song.

What materially affected the nature of German song was the termination of the honoured convention of figured bass (the harpsichordist made up his accompaniment according to a row of figures, suggesting the essential harmony, set below the bass line) and the replacement of the harpsichord by the piano. This, for reasons already stated, brought the accompaniment into greater prominence and, eventually, equalised the roles of voice and keyboard in song-with-keyboard-accompaniment. The process of adjustment was under way quite early in the second part of the eighteenth century. There are songs (especially some fine settings of Ramler's version of the Psalms) by Carl Philipp Emanuel Bach, and also by his distant cousin, Johann Ernst Bach, of Eisenach, that, from the point of design and texture are almost definable as *Lied* in the accepted sense of this word.

The ultimate determinant of *Lied*, however, was not so much this or that composer as Goethe, whose recreation of German lyrical poetry set off a whole train of reactions.

After Goethe came a great flood of lyrical poetry (not to mention drama) that was, in fact, the foundation of German, and European, Romanticism in its many phases. The whole of what has been discussed in Chapter 5 may be studied at source in German song of the nineteenth century. Through this century runs the main list both of major and minor poets – Goethe, Schiller (from whose works also a very large number of opera libretti derived), Eichendorff, Rückert (out of whose poems came Mahler's *Kindertotenlieder*), Müller, Lenau (Hungarian-born but a German writer), Heine, Mörike, and so on, to whom there were added (as kind of honorary members) Shakespeare, Burns, Byron, Thomas Moore, and, sometimes, Shelley. The aim of the song-writer of the nineteenth century was not so much to analyse texts, still less to use words as a vehicle for vocal virtuosity, but to convey "feeling". A fair enough aim, but difficult to achieve simply because of the attraction of techniques already proved in other men's works.

The apparatus of music made it possible for such an operation to be undertaken, however, with reasonable chance of success. A vocabulary of musical gestures (melodic pattern, accompanimental figurations, and harmonic formulas) had been accumulated that was more than adequate for the intensification of feelings and moods implicit in poetry. Since Romantic poetry was, by definition, rather less than precise it was ready made for translation into music. It is seldom that poetry can be lyrical in this sense. One of the rare periods in which it was was the nineteenth century – when literature aspired to embrace the virtues of music just as music attempted to become more specifically and obviously literary – which is why the *Lied* came when it did.

Now many composers tried to achieve a symbiosis of words and music, and there are thousands of Romantic songs that exhibit the difficulties inherent in the attempt. The songs of Mendelssohn (than whom few knew more about literature) are not in the first class. Nor are those of Robert Franz. Nor are those of Liszt. Those of Schubert, Schumann, and Brahms are; for in different ways these masters understood that songwriting was not merely setting words to music, but allowing the mood and colour of words to find their own level in the collateral textures of music. This means that the greatest songs of the *Lied* tradition are to be taken in as a whole, that is of a word-music entity. The listener is, therefore, advised to read the words of a song beforehand and to allow its performance to reinforce the general impressions he may retain after having read and put aside the text. Any attempt to look at words in detail and to listen at the same time, is ill advised since it separates the words from their new and proper situation. The idea that a song is a "story" set to music is too naïve in respect of the great songs, in connection with which it will be remembered that music is not a natural narrative medium.

Because of its nature the *Lied* is distinguished by a highly personal quality, and its psychological suggestiveness is considerable. It is the vehicle of the human situation, appreciated on the you-me level, of the nineteenth century, and the optimism of the first phase of the Romantic era eventually gives way to the pessimism of Brahms, of Strauss, and of Mahler. At the beginning of the era the emphasis was on life (nature, young love, joyful evocation of a past that is there to be relived); at the end it was on death. The end, however, was in the beginning. Schubert had his preoccupation with death, conveniently symbolised in "Death and the Maiden", but without sense of morbidity.

The *Lied* is a German term because the form which it represents was perfected by Germans and Austrians, but gradually it came to have a more or less generic significance. So that in essentials it was applicable to almost any solo sung with piano accompaniment, whether by Tchaikovsky, or Grieg, or Parry. The style of a Romantic song of this order was, however, often infected by national idiom. Sometimes consciously, sometimes unconsciously; sometimes with reference to, and even free arrangement of, folk-song, and sometimes with an awareness of atmosphere. The reflection of national idioms and ideals is particularly marked on both levels, in the songs of Borodin and Mussorgsky, and in those of Falla, where the evocative quality of the piano accompaniment is of a rare felicity.

Song, of course, is a complex art, being the junction of two; and yet, since speech is, in itself, essentially song there is a fundamental unity. In the first place – that is in the recesses of folk-song – the song is the singer, and the singer the song. From this there developed the whole separate tradition of music drama, or opera. From this also derived the principle of the importance of "interpretations". Good interpretation is that which makes of song a living entity, and in respect of the songs of the romantic tradition great gifts of insight are called for. Certainly one expects to be made aware of personality – but not the personality of the singer so much as of the composite poet-composer-singer personality while there is sure to be one or more facets of one's own personality.

Opera, of course, is song, but, being more involved and more complicated, lies on one side of solo song as we have seen it. On the other lies the general stock of choral music. Opera and choral music are two aspects of ritualised song, and sprang from common origins. Choral music is song which usually is seen to be relevant to a community rather than to an individual. In the western tradition the origins of choral music were liturgical, and the patterns of liturgy still exert at least a considerable fascination for composers. The centre of the western liturgy was the Mass, the durability of the poetical structure of which has outlived the doctrines out of which it was formed.

The five main sections of the Mass are – Kyrie, Gloria, Credo, Sanctus, Agnus Dei – and they provide a ready-made, unified, framework around which music may be assembled. The Requiem Mass, the Mass for the dead, adds to the scheme highly evocative hymns – *Requiem aeternam, Dies irae, Lux aeterna*, and, sometimes, *Libera me*. In the Mass is recorded the myth (anthropologically speaking) that for many centuries raised the hopes and stilled the fears of western man. When ritualised, according to ecclesiastical prescription, the myth was turned into an art-form, partly dramatic, partly musical. The first stage of the art-form gave the plainsong mass; the next stage gave the polyphonic mass. Thereafter the subject was adapted to whatever musical means were available.

Towards the musical setting of the Mass two attitudes have inevitably developed. Thus it is on the one hand seen as necessarily subject to the limitations of the liturgy, and to be subordinate to the doctrinal purposes of the dramatic-philosophic exegesis that is the service of the Mass; on the other as an expansion of the themes, of universal significance, that are represented by the poetry of the rite. Settings of the former kind (most, but not all, of the polyphonic era, and later examples, such as that of Stravinsky, deliberately tailored to utility) are only properly to be heard in context and with some sense of dedication and conviction. Settings of the latter kind, however, escape the limitations of "sacred music" and take their place in the general repertoire as contributions to a means of exploring the recesses of human nature.

In fact most Masses of the post-Reformation era are humanistic, if for no other reason than that the Church which gave them birth was also humanistic. To denote the Masses of Haydn and Mozart as worldly does not diminish their stature. Both composers absorbed into the tradition something of the richness of the world, Haydn with the deliberate intention of enriching the repertoire of the Faith. The symphonic-operatic impulses that went into the religious music of these composers – nowhere to more moving effect than in the *Requiem* that Mozart left to be finished by his pupil Sussmäyr – expanded into the vast proportions of Beethoven's *Missa Solemnis*. This, the tragedy and glory of the world as well as of a God, turns over the proposition that if God could become man then man could also become God (such was the scale of Beethoven's thinking).

The poetry of the Mass – as indeed all the poetry that is the basis of religious experience – is effective either because of its philosophic content or because of its immediately evocative properties. The visual element is a powerful means of communication. In former times it was translated into the paintings and sculptures that are among the masterpieces of art and among the principal acheivements of civilisation. In the German tradition of settings of the Mass (the Lutherans retained the Kyrie and Gloria of the pre-Reformation church) and Passion, a fusion of biblical narrative and the emotional associations inherent in the relevant section of the Credo of the Mass, the frequently expressionistic quality of the music is to be directly referred to the same quality as evinced in hundreds of carvings of the Man of Sorrows, and of the Crucifixion. Bach, like his Thuringian and Saxon predecessors, was brought up amid such art-works and their effect may be deduced from the agonies of the "Crucifixus" of the *B Minor Mass* and the profundity of the tragedy of the *St. John* and *St. Matthew Passions*. (It may be noted that there was a strong artistic talent in the Bach family, which came out in several generations of the Meiningen branch and also in J. S. Bach's grandson, also named Johann Sebastian the second son of Carl Philipp Emanuel, who was a professional painter.)

The connection between painting and drama in Italy was one of the reasons for the growth of opera (no-one who has studied sets for operas across the centuries will underrate the visual factor in this art-form). It is impossible to be unaware of this in listening to the religious works of Verdi. The *Requiem*, theatrical in the best sense, is a sublime essay in the presentation of the medieval view (to which Verdi as a simple Italian Catholic unquestioningly adhered) of the pains of death, the Last Judgement, and the final reconciliation of purified man with God. The *Requiem*, however, is more than this: it is a public monument, having been conceived as a tribute to the great Italian writer Alessandro Manzoni. Verdi's *Requiem* was first performed in 1874, a year after Manzoni's death, in St Mark's Church, Milan – with singers from the opera, a specially selected choir of 120 members and a hand-picked orchestra of 120 players. The work was received with enthusiasm.

Some fourteen years after Verdi's *Requiem* Gabriel Fauré, Organist of the Church of the Madeleine, in Paris, also produced a *Requiem Mass*. This, one of the most beautiful and serene works in the repertory of latter-day sacred music, philosophically speaking is a complete contrast to Verdi's work. The vindictiveness of the judicial processes of the Old Testament God (which is fully exposed by Verdi, as also by Elgar in *The Dream of Gerontius*) is virtually eliminated and the dominant note is one of tenderness. Fauré, Mlle. Nadia Boulanger suggested in *La Revue Musicale* in 1922, "understood religion more after the fashion of the tender passages in the Gospel according to St John, following St. Francis of Assisi rather than St. Bernard or Bossuet."

The Catholic and picturesque tradition of religious teaching is a constituent element in all religious music of large proportion, and without it such works as *The Dream of Gerontius* and Walton's *Belshazzar's Feast*, would hardly have come into existence. Yet these two works (as, of course, many others) represent the later stages of another tradition – that which, vaguely, is called the "Oratorio tradition". This tradition, its roots in the medieval play-with-music known as the "mystery", stemmed directly from an ecumenical union of Italian style and Protestant morality.

German protestantism in its Lutheran form centred on the chorale – the music of the community. Affiliated with the old style motet it formed the basis of the general choral tradition, that was largely instituted through Luther's educational principles. In the seventeenth century aesthetic interests brought together Italian cantata and German chorale-motet, the result of this marriage being the church cantata. The church cantatas of Bach (the Oratorios, so-called, and *Passions*, belong to this genre), to texts by Neumeister, Franck, Picander, Marianne von Ziegler, and others, were tilted towards instruction by the relationship between text and the particular significances of the liturgical calendar and the musical symbolism employed, and extended to general use by means of the chorales in which (when they could) the congregation participated.

The feature of the German cantata was the strong element of choral music, disposed in large concerto-like movements, as the opening of the *Christmas Oratorio*, in elaborate counterpoint, as that of the Kyrie of the *Mass in B Minor*, in dramatic interjections such as punctuate the *Passions*, or in extensive chorale-prelude-type choruses of the nature of the elaborate first movement of the *St. Matthew Passion*. The intensive introspection of much of this music, the transference of doctrinal tenets to philosophical observation in music (i.e. in the dialectical method that is counterpoint), establishes its essential character. It is this same character that re-emerges in the *Requiem*, as well as in the motets, of Brahms. The quest for intellectual sublimity through choral music affected many composers, in many countries, where the so-called Bach revival really got under way. Nowhere more than in Britain, where the works of Hubert Parry show the influence to a marked degree. The *Songs of Farewell*, splendidly composed for unaccompanied voices, are worthy to be set beside the finest of Brahms's motets. *Blest Pair of Sirens* a more extrovert essay in choral sonorities (Parry was, above all, an extrovert – and therefore a rarity among composers of this period), is a richly textured setting of Milton's *At a Solemn Music* which established itself from the start as a quintessentially English choral type piece. Which brings us to the specific contribution of the English to the general structure and purpose of choral music.

As elsewhere in Europe the English choral tradition was nurtured in the Church and, by means of various compromises, stepped over the Reformation with little disturbance of its essential character. The motet became the anthem, and Latin gave way to English. By the end of the Purcellian era the anthem (and its collateral "service") having acquired French and Italian characteristics – notably in respect of solo interludes and instrumental accompaniment, was of ample proportions. The splendid anthems of Purcell, Blow and Croft, that were performed in St. Paul's Cathedral after its opening in 1694, were well thought of, but more as exhibitions of musical genius than as examples of religious fervour. At the beginning of the eighteenth century, in England, it would in any case have been difficult to define what, if indeed it existed, religious fervour was.

Later in the century such definition was easier after the revitalising impact of Wesleyan teaching, which reinforced an already growing charitable altruism that found expression in the foundation of orphanages and hospitals and of Charities for the alleviation of many different forms of distress.

All these loose ends, musical and social alike, were caught up by the immigrant Handel and tied together in the most famous, if not most characteristic of his oratorios. There is a general notion that Handel is easy to understand. This I think not to be so. Certainly, the style, clean-cut, direct, impatient of unnecessary complexity, is direct and without impediment; but the content of the music, all-embracing, leaves few minds undisturbed. As history has proved, Handel has affected more people in more countries than any other of the great composers. This is because of his universality, a quality rooted in his profound understanding of the human voice. It is, for a start, difficult to find any music, whether for solo voice or for chorus, that is more singable than that of Handel.

Now Handel was bred to the fine German choral tradition,

and the solidity of his choral textures, and the energy of his counterpoint comes directly therefrom. To be precise, part of the chorus "Lift up your heads", in *Messiah*, is lifted more or less directly from a motet on the same text by the Leipzig Cantor, Sebastian Knüpfer, while the melodic line of the words "... and peace on earth" from "Glory to God" is the same as in a late seventeenth century motet, also to this same text, by an anonymous Thuringian composer. Eventually this tradition met up with the separate and independent English tradition, with which Handel became acquainted on his arrival in London, through his friendship with the singers of the Chapel Royal and St. Paul's Cathedral, through his study of the existing English repertoire, and through his early commissions to write Services, odes, and anthems. But there was another factor. In between leaving Germany and coming to England Handel had acquired an impeccable Italian style during a three-year stint in Italy. He was distinguished as a composer of Italian opera, and of cantatas and oratorios after the Italian manner.

He came to England to provide the aristocracy with Italian operas (as well as much other music) but ended up by writing non-Italian operas (but not in name), without action and with much emphasis on the chorus, to texts taken mostly (not exclusively) from biblical sources, which were defined ultimately as oratorios. *Messiah* was composed in 1741 (Handel had been in England by now for almost thirty years) and first performed by a team of soloists picked by Handel, by an orchestra led by the one-time London prodigy Matthew Dubourg, and by the combined choirs of the Cathedrals of Christ Church and St. Patrick, in the city of Dublin, on April 13, 1742. This, let it be said, was no mammoth-scale performance. There were about forty singers, and a small Baroque orchestra of trumpets, oboes, bassoons, drums, strings, harpsichord (from which the composer directed the performance), and organ.

Messiah, its operatic origins evident in the recitatives and arias and in the eye-catching music of the "Pastoral Symphony", its conjunction of English and German attitudes implicit in the choruses, established itself during the last seventeen years of

Handel's life not only as a popular musical entertainment, but also as a kind of eighteenth century morality. It stirred charitable emotion and out of its performances the majority of the hospitals of the age in Britain were financed. It also stimulated the foundation of choral societies and with the institution of these *Messiah* became the keystone of middle- and working-class musical culture. This was the case not only in Britain, but ultimately all over Europe and in the United States.

To accommodate the quite different forces from those which Handel himself had known the orchestration of *Messiah* (and other oratorios, and even, in due course, of Bach's *St. Matthew Passion*) was inflated. The first to re-arrange Handel's score was Mozart, for his Handel-loving patron, Baron van Swieten; throughout the nineteenth century many had a go at making Handel's music sound as it was thought he would have liked it to have sounded if he had lived in a later period. The present trend (except in places unblessed by those obedient to musicological disciplines) is towards a cleaned-up Handel – with *Messiah* as he might have performed it. Hence the differences between various recordings of the work.

Haydn came to London in 1791–2, noted the English enthusiasm for oratorio, and heard a Handel Festival. Three years later he was back again, and, reinforced in his belief that oratorio after the Handelian manner presented him with a challenge, went back to Vienna and composed *The Creation* which, when first performed in the Schwarzenberg Palace, proved an immediate success. So it was too in England, where the choruses, splendid in their colouring and endearing to the mass of amateur choral singers by reason of their energy and their practicability, were added to those of *Messiah* (and *Judas Maccabaeus*, etc.) as compulsory set-pieces in the choral repertoire.

Throughout the Victorian era the major industrial cities of Britain became major centres of choral music. None was more important than Birmingham, where the Triennial Festival (started in 1768 in the wake of Handelian fashion) became internationally important. In 1846 the third great and universally popular oratorio of the English tradition – also composed by a

German – was first performed in Birmingham Town Hall at the Festival of that year. This was Mendelssohn's *Elijah*, a work of immense dramatic power which revived the combative thrust of Handel's great studies of Old Testament heroics though not quite free of the sentimentality (e.g. "O rest in the Lord") that seeped out from under the fallen leaves of the first harvests of Romanticism. The drawing-room song (the *Lied* in degeneration) and ballad insinuated itself into the oratorio tradition. In the second half of the nineteenth century many bad oratorios, as well as secular cantatas (so-called) on heroic, jingoistic, and occasionally fantastic, themes, were fed into the English-speaking choral tradition. Against these, however, stood the choral works of Handel, Haydn, Mendelssohn, Beethoven, Mozart (the Masses being popularised by the use of inoffensive though often inept English words), Schumann (through the popularity of his widow in England), and the masterpieces of Bach.

Parry was an important figure in the choral world, in that he restored first principles: of directness of melodic line, vitality of rhythm, and agreement of verbal with musical expression. Parry helped to redeem choral music from inertia. In this sense his *Blest Pair of Sirens*, was epochal. But not so much as Elgar's *Dream of Gerontius*, which was performed for the first time at the Birmingham Festival on October 3, 1900. The first performance was indifferent and it was only the perceptive who immediately recognised a masterpiece. That it was a masterpiece was confirmed by Richard Strauss some eighteen months later after a performance of the work at Düsseldorf. Since then *Gerontius* has become an indisputable part of the English experience of music.

A setting of the famous poem by Cardinal Newman (the manuscript score reposes in the Oratory in Birmingham of which Newman was a member) *Gerontius* releases all those feelings that had been inhibited by the strictures and proprieties of Victorian musical methods. It is, so to speak, Elgar's study of "death and transfiguration", with the passage from life to death and beyond symbolised by the habiliments of Catholic doctrine which, however, are shown as significant in the world and outside the pew. Who was Gerontius? Elgar answered that. "I imagined," he wrote, "Gerontius to be a man like us . . ." Thus the oratorio, hinging on a skilful use of *Leitmotiv*, spontaneous as Verdi, many-coloured in its immaculately placed sonorities, is an account of the spiritual state of mankind on the edge of the unknown.

When Handel composed oratorios he was inspired by the techniques of the theatre. The greater oratorios were all within sight of opera. A composer in England, until recent years, was unlikely to get much satisfaction out of composing operas because of the remoteness of the likelihood of adequate performance. Elgar put his great dramatic genius into his choral works and in so doing renewed a general interest in oratorio as a dramatic medium. Of twentieth century works that which most vividly realises drama through oratorio is William Walton's *Belshazzar's Feast*. Here again there is no truck with sentiment, or with preconceptions concerning propriety. This work, intense in its rhythms and its dissonances, and splendiferous in its often overpowering instrumentation, is a vision of the barbarous opulence, the superstition, and the cruelty of a pagan court of the Middle East in biblical times. It is, in fact, the world of Handel's *Belshazzar*, or Strauss's *Salome*, but in unmistakeably twentieth century musical language. A Leeds Festival commission of 1931 *Belshazzar's Feast* was once thought improper for Anglican Cathedral performance (as also was an unexpurgated *Gerontius*). Since that time, however, it has taken its place in the select repertoire of major choral works that, rightly, are inevitable and regular selections for festival performance.

10

Music for the Theatre

THERE is, I suppose, no higher pleasure than to hear music in
the theatre, whether in conjunction with opera, operetta,
"musical" (a hybrid), or ballet. Not to put too fine a point on it,
music in this environment encourages a belief in its own realistic
virtues while, at the same time, releasing the listener-spectator
from the immediate obligations of reality and inducing him to
re-creation in the uplands of his imagination. This is nowhere
more evident than in the notable and familiar examples of
"incidental" music for plays, which include Mendelssohn's
Music (a whole suite after the Overture) for *A Midsummer
Night's Dream*, Grieg's *Peer Gynt* music, and Bizet's
L'Arlésienne pieces, all of which are evocative yet apparently
self-sufficient.

A play-with-music, in whatever form, is, of course, a fiction,
and it is precisely those qualities which underlie fiction *per se*,
that attract the general run of enthusiastic opera-goers – those,
that is, who are without specific or specialised interests. The
opera hero or heroine, or villain, is a surrogate, a symbol. There,
but by the Grace of God, go I, observes the Pinkertonian male
in view of the unfortunate, but ravishing Butterfly; or he of
Figaro propensities bemused by the flirtatious vivacity of
Susanna. In the nicest possible way it has to be made plain that
the primary attraction of opera (and its collaterals) is sex-
appeal.

Having come to terms at least with the term, opera is now by
way of being restored to the English-speaking world. The
process is a slow one (for opera production is an expensive
undertaking) and – despite valorous regional endeavours –

largely confined to capital cities. For nine out of ten who read this book opera (except for relatively rare exhibitions on television) is likely to mean recorded opera: in a sense, a disembodiment of a disembodiment, a Platonic dual remove from "reality".

Now since theatre-music is, in an absolute sense, incomplete in itself, it stands to reason that in listening to it the listener must supply some of the elements that are necessarily missing. Obviously, in the first place, the lack of the visual has to be compensated for. Fortunately since all experience is basically subjective it is not altogether impossible to make the necessary adjustment. But one should be aware that it needs to be made. An opera is to be seen and heard, and in hearing one should learn to see.

The libretto, or fiction, which is the basis of opera is, of course, a blue-print for action (which is where it differs from the literature from which it may be derived) and the function of operatic music is to give credibility to the many actions that add up to plot. Since the action within a libretto is localised, both temporally and topographically, it is also the function of music to convey a sense of time and place. This applies even when the libretto apparently lies outside both time and place, as in most of the Wagnerian music-dramas.

The history of opera is long and complicated. Rooted in folk-drama, and the derivant of folk-drama that became the medieval ritual music-drama of mystery and miracle-play, it is an art-form that in the widest sense is ritualistic: so much so that in the final computations of Wagnerian philosophy it became once more as a religion. In an era which has seen the decline of the age-old validities of official religion opera has been up-graded in the general estimation. Hence the enormous spread of interest in it in its manifold forms.

What one must be aware of in the English-speaking world is the fact that for centuries opera lay largely under theological interdict. The Puritans saw to it that it was excluded from the common pleasures. For nearly three hundred years such operas as have been performed in England have, for the most part, been importations (from Italy and Germany, mainly) and reserved to more or less select, and unrepresentative, audiences. In Italy and Germany, the principal opera-producing countries, opera was built into the main stream of social development, thereby acquiring a purposefulness within the national consciousness that in England is only paralleled by that appertaining to football. (It is notable that in England programmes of football matches are as lavish as those issued for opera performances on the continent, while the hand-outs for most continental football matches are as flimsy and uninspiring as those which more often than not are to be purchased at an English opera production.) In short, I am not sure that even yet the English and the Americans have come round to the idea that opera is to be enjoyed. If this were the case then operetta, virtually unknown in England and America, would be more happily placed than it is. The operative word is enjoyment: there is a lot to be said in favour of *enjoying* opera. One can make a start at home. The advantage of listening to recorded music in private is that one does not, as in public, have to keep up a social appearance by having to seem to be intelligent.

Opera is a collective word. Immediately and familiarly it breaks down into categories – "serious" opera (*opera seria*), "comic" opera (*opera buffa*), "grand" opera (a vague term and only of popular significance), "ballad" opera. Each category divides into other categories, according to definitions stated in previous chapters. These definitions help somewhat in establishing points of reference; thus the character of the voice parts is different in Romantic from classical opera, while the orchestral function is similarly qualified by considerations of general musical style. There is a wide spread of attitude towards characterisation which devolves from the confluence of musical style and social fashion.

In Baroque *opera seria* the characters are figures of myth and heroic legend, nobler and larger than life, yet symptomatic of the basic need of the aristocracy that the aristocrat, endowed with godlike qualities, is larger than life. In *opera buffa* the servant is the necessary antithesis to the aristocratic hero, to be laughed at. When the servant, as in Mozart, came to the point where he could be laughed at, the old values were under siege.

The supernatural in opera was challenged by the natural, and in due course realism, or *verismo*, came into vogue. The hot breath of life exudes from, for instance, *Carmen, La Traviata, Tosca, Cavalleria Rusticana*. It is the more robust, and warm-blooded, among operas that have found a permanence in the international repertoire that is not always warrantable on musical grounds alone.

But opera is not music alone: it is music *plus* a number of other elements, which are present in varying strength.

The opera tradition was pre-empted by the Italians during the first expansive quarter of the seventeenth century. A zeal for the glories that were Greece settled libretti on the classical stories of Daphne and Apollo, and Orpheus and Euridice; progressive theories concerning the function of music in relation to words established the narrative convenience of recitative and aria; enthusiasm for spectacle had as by-product evocative instrumental music. By mid-century the cult of Italian *opera seria* had become a popular as well as an aristocratic cult in Italy, with particular traditions established in particular towns, and, inevitably, it had spread across Europe. The first great composer of opera that is now publicly viable was Monteverdi. The second great Italian master was Alessandro Scarlatti, whose refinement of vocal line and sublimation of the techniques of *bel canto* set the seal of the singer on Italian opera apparently for all time.

Italian opera is essentially an exhibition of singing skills, an act of faith in the capacity of the human voice to convey emotions more powerfully than any other medium. The great Italian operas were built round great singers – from Cuzzoni (of Handelian fame) to Callas, from Strada del Pò, whose superb voice unhappily issued from a graceless figure, to Giuseppina Strepponi, not only the mistress of song but also of Giuseppe Verdi, and the inspiration of the part of Abigaille in *Nabucco*. The great Italian composers of opera – among whom the familiar names are those of Monteverdi, Alessandro Scarlatti, Pergolesi, Cimarosa, Donizetti, Bellini, Rossini, and Verdi – were without peers in their treatment of the voice as a musical instrument. To this talent was added, in various degrees, that of achieving dramatic credibility.

Because the Italian school did concentrate so whole-heartedly on the voice, and because the set-piece aria (preceded by recitative) was a congenial means of accommodating the singer excerpts from Italian are more viable outside the theatre than selections from many other forms of opera. In fact, the criticism of Italian opera at any rate in the eighteenth century was that it was often little more than a concert in costume. Nonetheless, because Italian composers worked in the theatre they rarely lacked the capacity to endow music with a palpable theatrical quality. This remained constant, though adapting itself to the varying theatrical conventions of successive periods.

So far as the record-collector is concerned it is likely that Italian *opera seria* of the Baroque era will be represented – by excerpts from if not by complete works – by the operas of Handel. In respect of opera Handel showed that it was possible for a non-Italian to master the Italian style. (He was neither the first nor the last foreigner to do this.) It so happens that among Baroque opera composers Handel is the best bet for a live performance, and the fact that his operas are staged with increasing frequency (not only in Germany, where they have been constantly staged over the past half-century, but also in Britain and the United States) is a tribute not only to their musical quality but also to their dramatic power. It should be recognised from the oratorios (operas in other guise) that Handel had the supreme dramatico-musical gift of being able to make characters live, primarily through the incredible communicative force of his melodic lines. Simply because he possessed the psychological insight to understand the problems of the distressed, the deranged, the jealous, to balance these against the exuberances of the normal and the pride of the powerful, and to translate his insights into musical form Handel rode over the restrictions imposed on him by the artificial structure of the then *opera seria*. It is with the fuller associations of opera in mind that we should listen to the oratorios, which, being operas *minus* spectacle and action, and so intended, are an ideal exercise for the listener in supplying what is not there!

There were those who delighted in sending-up *opera seria*, partly for social and partly for artistic reasons. In Italy the

162

obverse of *opera seria* was *opera buffa*, which immediately stemmed from the disinclination of (especially) Neapolitan opera-goers to sit through a whole evening of uplift. Interspersed between the Acts of *opera seria* were comedy interludes, or *intermezzi*, based on low life rather than high life – or, as in the classic instance of intermezzo, Pergolesi's *La serva padrona*, on situations involving both. In that *opera buffa* brought opera down to ground level – another splendid example according to the Pergolesi prescription is *Pimpinone*, by Telemann, who like Handel could adopt and adapt an Italian style when he wished – it was in some respects, although comic, more serious than serious opera.

There were other branches of musico-dramatic art on the outskirts of opera. The English had a preference for plays with incidental songs and incidental music. Hence the long list of non-operas by Purcell with one incidental and accidental masterpiece of through-composed music-drama, *Dido and Aeneas*, and the ballad sequence arranged round the startling realism and satire of *The Beggar's Opera* – the work whose popularity from 1728 onwards spelt disaster for imported *opera seria*. This homely tradition (to which Johann Christian Bach contributed when he lived in London) was persistent, passing through Thomas Augustine Arne, whose Shakespeare songs are among the major inspirations of English music, and a series of minor composers, into the conjoint works of Gilbert and Sullivan, and, beyond, into the modern musical.

At the point at which the "Savoy" operas hit London the native English ballad opera, which had touched Romantic opera in the now forgotten works of Stephen Storace and Edward Loder, drew inspiration from the separate strain of French operetta, satirical and parodistic, and perfected by Offenbach. Sullivan, Anglo-Irish, was a master craftsman (until they disagreed his understanding of Gilbert's requirements both as librettist and stage director was absolute), but also a composer whose genius as such has hardly been recognised. Behind him lay his incidental music for *The Tempest*, in no way inferior to Mendelssohn's Shakespeare music, and a fine "Irish" Symphony. Turned aside from greater projects by the exigencies of English musical life his association with Gilbert was his salvation. The "Savoy" operas are compounded of Italian (bel canto), German, (orchestral) and French (opera bouffe) elements, without which they would not have been so characteristically English. For the satire on public institutions that is their strength depended on the composer's objectivity. This was ensured by the quality of his musicianship. The genre operetta was an important one, and the catalyst in the nineteenth century was Offenbach, whose influence will appear at a later point in this survey. For the moment let it be said that Sullivan's certainty of theatrical touch had not been experienced in English music since the days of Purcell – who also was under obligation to a French tradition.

A devotee of Purcell recognises in him a marvellous composer of dance music, to which he was more or less drawn by the French style that was popularised in England by Charles II. This monarch had, while languishing in exile at the Court of France, correctly determined that Lully, the chief composer to Louis XIV, was on the right lines in emphasising the charms of ballet. Lully, of course, was obeying the instructions of his master, but in so doing he laid the foundations of ballet, both as an independent art-form and as an adjunct to opera. Moreover, by moderating the excesses of Italian *coloratura* style and relying on the more direct quality of French *chanson*, he sounded a warning to those who considered that in opera music was more important than the words from which it was created. Lully was the contemporary and colleague of Pierre and Thomas Corneille, and of Molière and Racine, whose dramatic gifts carried far into the history of music in that many operas of later time have libretti based on their works.

There is a frequent feeling that it is a good thing to know what an opera is about. This feeling is by no means unreasonable. So far as the classic themes, e.g. of Orpheus and Euridice, are concerned, it is theoretically supposed that those who are sufficiently educated will know the story anyway. Even in the eighteenth century those who were supposed to often didn't, while those who were not supposed to often showed their resentment at the pretensions of their superiors. Hence the rough treatment handed out by the English to Italian opera singers, and the cultivation of some kind of music-drama in the vernacular. In Germany a form of play-with-music somewhat analogous to the English ballad-opera (both stemmed from a common theatrical tradition of the sixteenth century) was called *Singspiel*. Bach's *Peasant Cantata*, a bucolic comedy with folk-songs and parody songs stitched in, was almost a *Singspiel*. In due course this tradition had important consequences for opera at large through the inheritance of the tradition by Mozart.

A composer of music for the theatre is required to be more than a composer. In one sense, of course, he may be less than a composer. What matters is that he should know the theatre, and the peculiar relationship between stage and auditorium. The masters of opera (and there were many) of the first part of the eighteenth century understood quite well that essentially opera was song. At the same time the importance of spectacle was enhanced, first by the development of ballet, second by technical advances in respect of stage machinery. The French dancer, Sallé, who was engaged for various works of Handel, including *Alcina*, for the season 1734-5, in order to give a boost to the box-office, popularised ballet through her effrontery in performing in what for those days was akin to striptease manner. In 1760 the Paris ballet-master Jean Noverre, catching on to Rousseau's principle of "return to nature", reformed and naturalised ballet through his *Lettres sur la danse*. This was the time when Gluck, discontented with the trivialities that passed as opera on the one hand, and impressed with the general idea of naturalism, was evolving his theories on the character of opera.

In brief, Gluck, who settled in Vienna in 1750 but was very much a European, brought the basic elements of opera into a new harmony, with the intention of achieving a verisimilitude that palpably was missing from the general run of both serious and comic operas. Verisimilitude in this connection refers rather to truth to emotional conditions than to the kind of musical journalism that was later to distinguish the *verismo* style.

Gluck's *Orfeo ed Euridice* was first performed in Vienna in 1762, but it was not until fourteen years later, when this opera (in a French version) and *Iphigénie en Aulide*, and *Alceste*, were performed in Paris, that it became clear that opera was moving into a new phase. Gluck, disregarding the conventions of Italian method, both simplified opera and deepened its significance. His was music of a passionate intensity, the stronger because of its economy of gesture, that heretofore, on this scale, had not been known.

The reforms of Gluck were epoch-making, leading into the romantic aspects of Mozart – as particularly in *Die Entführung aus dem Serail* (1782) and *Die Zauberflöte* (1791) – and through him to the fuller romanticism of Carl Maria von Weber; and also into the dramatic force of Cherubini's operas, and through these into Beethoven's *Fidelio*.

Mozart, acutely aware of the varieties of theatre music practised during his lifetime, summarised them in a series of works which crossed over every category without properly belonging to any. *Bastien und Bastienne* (1768) is described as a "German operetta", but tune-wise it picks up the French attitude to song that went into German song through a once-famous anthology of songs by the Leipzig poet-musician known as "Sperontes". *Idomeneo* belongs to the genre *opera seria*, but the characterisation with the music (especially of Ilia) and the extension of dramatic purpose to ensemble (as in the quartet of the third act) is far away from the general, easy, tradition. *Die Entführung* is a *Singspiel* by definition, but with a wit and refinement that were alien to that tradition. *Die Zauberflöte* also came at the behest of Schikaneder – a most experienced man of the theatre and himself, singer, librettist and composer – from the tradition of the popular theatre, from *Singspiel* and pantomime. Yet by this investment of his finest music in this work Mozart, unconsciously, lifted the whole of opera to a new philosophical level. *Die Zauberflöte*, subject of a thousand theses, is all-embracing – it is both comedy and tragedy, it is instinct with mystery and magic, but also mysticism: it is, in short, what the listener cares to make of it. The plot, of course, is absurd; but then so too is life. *Figaro*, first performed in Vienna in 1786, highly successful but withdrawn after only nine performances, is the most captivating *opera buffa* in existence. Yet a work which is so plainly satirical (on which account the original text from Beaumarchais ran into censorship trouble in Vienna) is more than a mere comedy. It is comic in the Aristophanic sense, mocking the pretensions of humanity though with a compassion that is written into what in Mozart is simply defined as Mozartian. Figaro, like Don Juan (embodied also in Mozartian opera), Don Quixote, and Till Eulenspiegel, is much more than a character in a story. He is irreverence incarnate, and made immortal not only by Mozart but by Rossini, whose *Il Barbiere di Siviglia*, is one of the latest but also one of the finest examples of *opera buffa*. It is a sobering thought that when this work was first performed in Rome, in 1816, it was cried down by a public that for reasons that must now seem inadequate preferred an opera on the same subject by Paisiello.

If many streams converged in Mozart, so, after his death did many extend from him in different directions. German opera began its effective separate existence with him, while Italian opera, while retaining its basic principle of *bel canto* acquired a deeper sense of purpose. But, by the end of the century there hung over all the French Revolution, which exercised a profound influence on the future of opera, and sometimes, indeed, on the lives of composers.

Those who are acquainted with Cimarosa's masterpiece, *Il matrimonio segreto* (the high spot of the Viennese Opera season of 1792), will recognise in it a vivacity and felicity of style that is hardly inferior to that of Mozart. A closer scrutiny of this work reveals that Cimarosa, in guying the convention of the marriage market was in fact being equally critical as, if not more so than, Mozart, of the restrictions imposed by social convention on the liberty of the individual. It is to be noted that Cimarosa, unlike some, was unafraid otherwise to express his convictions. When the French armies entered Naples in 1799 he declared himself on their side, wherefore, afterwards, he was imprisoned. The aforesaid Paisiello, also declared for Napoleon and only escaped the fate of Cimarosa by taking refuge in Paris.

A greater sense of urgency came into Italian opera through

Donizetti and Bellini, whose impassioned interpretation of themes that not only had personal but also, on occasion, national interest (even if this was disguised), and genius for ecstatic melodic expression endeared them to audiences all over Europe. Bellini's *La Sonnambula*, a great lyric drama based on a libretto by Felici Romani (librettist also for Donizetti and Rossini), was much acclaimed by Wagner, not least of all for the fidelity of the musical expression to the nature of the plot. *I Puritani* is a testimony to the fascination exercised by the historic fiction of Walter Scott over Europe since it is based on Scott's *Old Mortality*. Donizetti's *Lucia di Lammermoor* – with the most famous study of madness in the whole of opera – is also taken from Scott.

Both these composers helped to bring back the libretto as the activating force in Italian opera, and without their vitality and melodic inventiveness the masterpieces of Rossini and Verdi would have been less probable.

During the early years of the nineteenth century opera – the most inherently romantic of all art forms and, therefore, that most suited to the Romantic era – became popular in the widest sense of the word (except in London, where native opera barely had a look in). Emotionally charged it increasingly became an emotional stimulant.

It was the emotional content of Cherubini's operas (of which *Les Deux Journées*, or *Der Wasserträger*, is known at least by its overture), as well as the originality of their orchestration, that commended them to German audiences. Cherubini was well represented in the theatre at Bonn when Beethoven was a boy, and the theme of emancipation in *Lodoïska* (the old theatrical "prison scene" took on a new significance when political tensions heightened) made a deep impression on Beethoven. *Lodoïska* was first performed in 1791, the year in which Mozart died. The story of *Fidelio*, based on a text by Cherubini's librettist Jean-Nicholas Bouilly, was indeed a re-working of some of the ideas already expressed in *Lodoïska*.

Of the plots of the heroic, mythic, operas, it used to be said (and still is) that they were universal. This, in the broad sense, is true. But the whole trend of human thought from the

Renaissance to the Romantic era was away from the universal towards the particular; from them to us, from us to me, from then to now. Opera increasingly proved a convenient repository for hopes and ambitions that, for obvious reasons, could not be expressed in directly political terms.

Fidelio is an exposition of the creed of the common man: I believe in freedom. The imprisoned Florestan – the contemner of tyranny – is a symbol. Leonora, his wife, whose disguise as the boy Fidelio gives the title to the opera, is also a symbol. So too are Pizarro, the tyrannical governor, and Rocco, the unwilling jailer. Plot and under-plot are not all that different from those of many of the classic operas that hinged on prison scenes. But in the early nineteenth century they took on a new significance, that increased throughout the nineteenth and reached a climax in the twentieth century. Beethoven's treatment of the theme, by means of all the symphonic resources at his disposal, ensured that the significance of the opera was made clear. The message is unmistakable – in the sequence of overtures (i.e. *Fidelio*, and three *Leonora* overtures) which Beethoven wrote at different times, in the characterisation of the principals, in the ensembles of which the quartet at the end of Act I, sc. I, is the consummation of both style and of feeling. Of all his works Beethoven loved this the best. The reason is not far to seek: *Fidelio* is the complete statement of his musico-philosophical beliefs.

Dealing with the particular rather than the general theme affected the whole course of opera. During the nineteenth century the realistic novel played an important part in directing the attention of composers to what was central to contemporary thought. Bizet's *Carmen* was based on Prosper Merimée's novel of that title; Puccini's *La Bohème* on Henri Murger's *Scènes de la vie de Bohème*, his *Tosca* on Victorien Sardou's drama, *La Tosca*, and his *Madam Butterfly* on a magazine story by David Belasco. Verdi's *La Traviata* was founded on *La Dame aux Camélias* by the younger Alexandre Dumas. Some of these works were journalistic in the sense that they were taken direct from life and from experience. In no pejorative sense the immediacy of the writing of Bizet, Puccini, and Verdi, suggests a journalistic talent finding outlet through a conjunction of boldness and simplicity. These composers were not ashamed to aim at the popular market, their achievement lay in their respect for this market. The popularisation of opera was on the one hand a consequence of a general raising of living standards and, on the other, a part of the popularisation of music.

The line of realism established in the theatre during the nineteenth century has been strongly etched into twentieth century music. But it is but one more strain in the multifarious character of opera. On the whole, in essentials, opera, being drama, and drama being founded on simple principles, is what it was. That is to say, it is either comedy or tragedy encapsuled within an entertainment that both defies and complements the actualities of existence. However realistic it may appear to be it is always at several moves from reality. Thus the non-Spaniard, the non-French, the non-Italian are carried away, sometimes nostalgically and in memory of holidays abroad, by the exotic qualities of the music of Bizet, Puccini, Verdi. While the chances of appreciating the full Brechtian social criticism that was the purpose of *Porgy and Bess* are likely to be obliterated by the piquancy and/or plaintiveness of Gershwin's melodic talent. Though perhaps merely by existing in the world repertoire, this, as yet unique, work exerts its influence.

Here we are on the outer circle of enjoyment, whirled into enchantment by (in the case of the present reader) the pressure of a needle. On we go, after all that has been observed on the side of realism, towards the scintillation of the Spanish idioms of Bizet, the glitter of Verdi's overtures and the enriching power of his endless, Mediterranean melodies, to the sentimentality that lies hardly hidden in the plangent lyrics of Puccini. What carries us along is, in fact, the music. Even more is this the case in respect of German nineteenth century opera, frequently with a gross improbability of libretto (as in Weber) or an opaqueness of plot (as, excepting *Die Meistersinger*, in the case in Wagner), where the music is all. There are, of course, exceptions: not very available and rarely performed in other countries are the delightful, homely operas of Albert Lortzing, replete with a typical bourgeois good-humour, and Nicolai's masterpiece, *The Merry Wives of Windsor*. For the life of me I cannot think why this latter, so Stratfordly Shakesperian, so unpretentious, and so warmly comic is not a best-seller outside of Germany. However, that is as may be; and in the meanwhile Wagner, the Grand Central of German nationalism, stands as the typical exemplar of German music. The word to cancel is "typical". Wagner, like Beethoven, was only himself, only more so. The would-be great musical architect of the cosmos he summarised the aspirations of Romantic Germany. Wagnerian music-drama was the conclusion of ideals that, in so far as a mystical union of thought and art was concerned, had begun to stir far back, even in the days of the Mastersingers. Observing the directions taken by Mozart (in the comedy of *Die Meistersinger*), by Gluck (in the union of elements into a consistent whole), by Weber (the mystical transference of scenery into sound observable in *Der Freischütz* and *Oberon* is achieved in, for instance, the river music of *Das Rheingold* and the forest music of *Siegfried*), by Beethoven, by Meyerbeer and Rossini (whose spectacular operas for Paris originated the term Grand Opera – to which genre Verdi's *Aida* also belongs), Wagner expanded the resources of music to accommodate his ambitions. Yet unlike, say, Meyerbeer, he never lost sight of the music. In the end the progenitor of modern music-drama was defeated by the enchantment of music itself. It was, by reason of his amplification of the musical resources of music-drama, that Wagner made out of German opera a liturgy that culminated in the cycle of *The Ring* (a kind of pagan counterpart to the seasonal church-cantata sequence of Bach's time) and, of course, in the ultimate, mythic, conclusion of *Parsifal*.

In a letter to Hugo von Hofmannsthal, written in 1913, Richard Strauss observed that "in art everything can only be done once". That, I suppose, is the final justification of the greatness of Mozart as a composer of opera. So far as Strauss himself was concerned there is, beyond doubt, one work of his that lives up to the standard of uniqueness he set before himself. That is *Der Rosenkavalier*, the one undisputed operatic masterpiece of the twentieth century. It is worth making the point that this work (of which the libretto was by von Hofmannsthal) is a twentieth century work, for in general the point will escape the listener whose prejudices concerning what is "modern" are liable to overcome his pleasure.

Of course, 1911, in which year *Der Rosenkavalier* was first performed at the Dresden Opera, is a world ago; but it still belongs to the twentieth century. At that time – Wagner having apparently closed one chapter in the history of musical style – composers, especially Debussy, Stravinsky, and Schoenberg, were in search of new channels of expression. Strauss, the most professional musician of the age, was less absorbed in theories of technique (he was a consummate master of techniques, particularly, being the son of a horn-player and himself a conductor, those of the orchestra) than in their practical application. In respect of opera he was both practical and impeccable. A Strauss opera "comes off" (with the possible exception of the allegory-laden *Die Frau ohne Schatten*) and, whereas one may listen to the symphonic poem, or dance-suite, excerpts from Wagner, one is obliged, I think, to listen to a Strauss work as a whole. This, of course, is possible, since Strauss did not out-step the natural limitations imposed by convention.

Der Rosenkavalier is a splendid comedy (from Mozart, by way of Lortzing and Nicolai), a study of eighteenth century high-life modes elevated to fairy-story by the love-symbol of the silver-rose and reduced to normality by the strength of the characterisation. It was a superb collaboration between librettist and composer that produced the unforgettable images of the Marschallin, of Baron Ochs, of Octavian, the young Count and "Cavalier of the Rose" (who is returned to a forgotten convention by being represented by a mezzo-soprano), and that set them and their intrigues in the happy land between Mozartian *buffa* and Viennese waltz.

Opera is a continuous process of absorption and rejection; always more than a mere "form" it is a living organism. On the one side it is the story of literature, on the other the encapsulisation of the whole of music. It is, I submit, the listener's most congenial guide to musical thought in general, since at no point is he away from the *terra cognita* of recognisable concepts. It is the firm ground on which he feels himself to "know what is going on."

Like every other living organism opera has a family organisation. The main branches of the family have been indicated, but, since its home is in the theatre, there are many more. It will not escape notice that many operas already mentioned incorporate dance as a contributory factor to plot development, or annotation. The waltzes in *Der Rosenkavalier* are a case in point. In the eighteenth century, dances, though always tending towards the ritual, were first introduced (as in the case of Handel) as a concession to popular taste. By the time we reach Rameau (in the line of descent from Lully operatically speaking) and Gluck (the "Elysian fields" music from *Orpheus* being a beautiful example) dances became functional, and an integral part of the whole. In the following period dances, still regarded as functional, were symbolic of one or two cults; on the one hand of the exotic, on the other of the nationalist. Hence the ballet episodes in the operas of Meyerbeer, of Wagner's *Tannhäuser* (put into Act II to accommodate French taste), *Die Meistersinger* (dance of apprentices), and *Parsifal* (dance of flowermaidens), of Borodin's Polovtsian girls in *Prince Igor*, and Strauss's *Salome* ("Dance of the Seven Veils").

The fascination of the human form is one of the inescapable features of any consideration of art, which, on one level, is what art is about. Thus the separate but cumulative development of ballet, which, for reasons which have at least been implied came into its own in the nineteenth century, especially in France where a ballet tradition had long been established. The eighteenth century ballet had moved towards "naturalism", by (literally) rather slow and deliberate steps. During the Romantic era – heralded ballet-wise by Fanny Elssler the ballerina daughter of Haydn's servant and amanuensis, who settled Spanish music in the European ballet scheme by her introduction of the Cachucha – romantic ideas concerning women in general led to the romanticism of the ballerina in particular. Thus she learned to look like, and to behave as, she was expected. Lightness, grace, provocation by careful devestment – the great pioneer was Taglioni – and so on, made ballet both fashionable and enticing. It was, at first, a minority of composers who took the art of ballet music seriously. When the gentlemen, especially of the Latin Quarter, went to see what they wanted to see they were sometimes less than particular as to what they heard. That their pleasure would be enhanced if they also heard what they saw was the inspiration of Léo Delibes, the lightness and ethereal quality of whose *Coppelia* (1870) and *Sylvia* (1876), may be taken as the starting-point of modern ballet. It was his enthusiasm for Delibes (an enthusiasm shared by Elgar, whose *Wand of Youth* music and, particularly, "Dorabella" of the "*Enigma*" *Variations* show many Delibes-like touches) that led Tchaikovsky seriously to explore the possibilities of ballet. So seriously, that Taneiev complaining that the Fourth Symphony was too much like ballet and too little like symphony, was sharply answered by Tchaikovsky. In one of his most interesting letters Tchaikovsky expanded on the theme: "I can never understand why 'ballet music' should be used as an epithet of contempt".

The truth was that before Tchaikovsky ballet had not been treated on a serious musical level in Moscow or St. Petersburg, and that it was only so regarded after the production of *Swan Lake*, *Sleeping Beauty*, and *The Nutcracker*, all of which annoyed the complacent among ballet-goers because the music, being considered so complicated took the mind off the stage. Known alone through excerpts in the form of Suites the pieces which Tchaikovsky wrote for these ballets deserves the closest attention; for moved, on the one hand, by the ethereal quality of the stories (Tchaikovsky, in many worldly ways immature, lived, Strephon-like, half etherealised) and, on the other by the fantasy of Russian legend, he achieved a new kind of mobility or plasticity of musical textures, out of which came the balletic art of Diaghilev and the consequent ballet scores of Debussy, Ravel, and Stravinsky. Ballet was an emancipation from opera. Much of the freedom of "modern" music is a consequence of the liberating impulse of ballet. Thus we are back where we started – at the rhythmic foundation of all music.

"You know," wrote Ravel to Jean Marnold in reference to *La Valse* which he described as a kind of memorial to Johann Strauss, "now I delight in those admirable rhythms, and that in my opinion the *joie de vivre* expressed in dance goes much deeper than the puritanism of César Franck." *Joie de vivre*, that is the quality that suffused Renaissance music and, indeed, made it Renaissance music. *Joie de vivre* is the inspiration of every great artistic movement. Movements, alas!, often end far from where they began – with a *joie de mourir*, or, on the cosmic scale, with a Twilight of the Gods. *Joie de vivre* is the proper beginning of revolt, a point well understood at the present time. Rebellious spirits let loose in the field of music tend to be overpraised for their demolition of forms and procedures: there were those, who by riding down the high seriousness of the hierarchy made, perhaps, an equally important contribution to the art of music and theatre.

The masters of Viennese waltz, the Strausses, not only immortalised the sociable virtues of Vienna, and of Austria, and propounded a more attractive thesis of existentialism than any other pseudo-philosophers, but ennobled and refreshed the province of what is now called light music. Johann Strauss, the younger, perfected the waltz, and (he was an admirer and supporter of Wagner) gave to it a sophistication derived from the general music of the middle nineteenth century that was the apt extension of the last splendours of Habsburg rule. In mid-career Strauss was greatly influenced by the pungent wit of Offenbach's operettas and, turning to operetta, produced the masterpieces that always threatened to break out of the un-inhibited romanticism endemic in the Austrian character. *Die Fledermaus*, produced at the Theater an der Wien in 1875, remains a monument to a bygone age, when good humour could still be recognised. The same warmth and gaiety characterises *Der Zigeunerbaron*, which caters for the armchair traveller by its Hungarian association. The culmination of Austro-Hungarian amity was in the operettas of Franz Lehár, who, Hungarian-born, lived most of his life in the idyllic spa of Bad Ischl near Salzburg, where he composed most of his 30 operettas, that include *Die Lustige Witwe* and the *Graf von Luxemburg*. These, the near reflection of an age gone beyond recall, stand as emblems of a *joie de vivre* that collapsed in the cataclysm of a continent.

What is enjoyment? In the end it is to share with Elgar the

belief that "the sun still seems to show us a golden 'beyond'." It may be out of fashion to say so; but the music that counts is the music that stimulates that belief. Much of this music has come from the environment of the theatre, and theatre music is a good point of departure for the musical pilgrim.

DISCOGRAPHY

The main list of records is based on references in the text to the principal works. A selection of these would form the basis of a collection. However, listed below are additional records covering music not mentioned in the book, but worthy of serious consideration for inclusion in a comprehensive record collection.

c/w indicates coupled with

SYMPHONIES

BEETHOVEN

No. 1 in C, Op. 21
(c/w Beethoven: No. 8)
   Philharmonia/Otto Klemperer   SAX2318/CX1554
No. 2 in D, Op. 36
(c/w Beethoven: "The Ruins of Athens" – incidental music)
   Royal Philharmonic/Sir Thomas Beecham   HQS1154
No. 3 in E flat, Op. 55 ("Eroica")
   BBC Symphony/Sir John Barbirolli   ASD2348
No. 5 in C minor, Op. 67
(c/w Beethoven: King Stephen Overture)
   Philharmonia/Otto Klemperer   SAX2373/CX1721
No. 6 in F, Op. 68 ("Pastoral")
   Berlin Philharmonic/André Cluytens   ASD433/ALP1863
Symphony No. 7 in A, Op. 92
   Philharmonia/Otto Klemperer   SAX2415/CX1769
No. 9 in D minor, Op. 125 ("Choral")
   Soloists/Philharmonia Orchestra and Chorus/Otto Klemperer
                                                  SAX2276–7/CX1574–5

BERLIOZ

Symphonie fantastique, Op. 14
   French National Radio/Sir Thomas Beecham   ASD399/ALP1633
Harold in Italy, Op. 16
   Yehudi Menuhin (viola)/Philharmonia/Colin Davis   ASD537/ALP1986

BRAHMS

No. 1 in C minor, Op. 68
   Vienna Philharmonic/Sir John Barbirolli   ASD2401
No. 2 in D, Op. 73
(c/w Brahms: Tragic Overture)
   Vienna Philharmonic/Sir John Barbirolli   ASD2421
No. 3 in F, Op. 90
(c/w Brahms: Academic Festival Overture)
   Philharmonia/Otto Klemperer   SAX2351/CX1536
No. 4 in E minor, Op. 98
   Philharmonia/Otto Klemperer   SAX2350/CX1591

BRUCKNER

No. 3 in D minor (1889 version)
   Vienna Philharmonic/Carl Schuricht   ASD/ALP2284
No. 4 in E flat ("Romantic")
   Philharmonia/Otto Klemperer   SAX2569/CX1928

DVOŘÁK

No. 9 (formerly No. 5) in E minor, Op. 95 ("From the New World")
(c/w Smetana: Vltava from "Ma Vlast")
   Berlin Philharmonic/Herbert von Karajan   SAX2275/CX1642

ELGAR

Symphony No. 1 in A flat, Op. 55
  Philharmonia/Sir John Barbirolli   **ASD540/ALP1989**
No. 2 in E flat, Op. 63
(c/w Elgar: Falstaff, Op. 68)
  Hallé/Sir John Barbirolli   **ASD610–1/ALP2061–2**

FRANCK

Symphony in D minor
  New Philharmonia/Otto Klemperer   **SAX/CX5276**

HAYDN

No. 45 in F sharp minor ("Farewell")
(c/w Mozart: Eine kleine Nachtmusik, etc.)
  Bath Festival/Yehudi Menuhin   **ASD506/ALP1955**
No. 98 in B flat
(c/w Haydn: No. 101 "Clock")
  Philharmonia/Otto Klemperer   **SAX2395/CX1748**
No. 100 in G ("Military")
(c/w Haydn: No. 99)
  Royal Philharmonic/Sir Thomas Beecham   **ASD339/ALP1693**
No. 103 in E flat ("Drum Roll")
(c/w No. 104 "London")
  Royal Philharmonic/Sir Thomas Beecham   **ASD341/ALP1695**

MAHLER

No. 2 in C minor ("Resurrection")
  Elisabeth Schwarzkopf, Hilde Rossl-Majdan, Philharmonia Chorus
  and Orchestra/Otto Klemperer   **SAX2473–4/CX1829–30**
No. 4 in G
  Elisabeth Schwarzkopf/Philharmonia/Otto Klemperer
        SAX2441/CX1793

MENDELSSOHN

No. 3 in A minor, Op. 56 ("Scotch")
(c/w Mendelssohn: Hebrides Overture)
  Philharmonia/Otto Klemperer   **SAX2342/CX1736**
No. 4 in A, Op. 90 ("Italian")
(c/w Schumann: No. 4 in D minor)
  Philharmonia/Otto Klemperer   **SAX2398/CX1751**

MOZART

No. 25 in G minor, K.183
(c/w Mozart: Eine kleine Nachtmusik, etc.)
  Philharmonia/Otto Klemperer   **SAX/CX5252**
No. 29 in A, K.201
(c/w Mozart: No. 33)
  New Philharmonia/Otto Klemperer   **SAX/CX5256**
No. 38 in D, K.504 ("Prague")
(c/w Mozart: 32 and 35 "Haffner")
  English Chamber Orchestra/Daniel Barenboim   **ASD2327**
No. 39 in E flat, K.543
(c/w No. 40 in G minor, K.550)
  English Chamber Orchestra/Daniel Barenboim   **ASD2424**
Symphony No. 41 in C, K.551 ("Jupiter")
(c/w Mozart: Divertimento No. 2)
  Royal Philharmonic/Sir Thomas Beecham   **HQM1117**

PROKOFIEV

No. 1 in D, Op. 25 ("Classical")
(c/w Stravinsky: The Rite of Spring)
  New Philharmonia/Rafael Frühbeck de Burgos   **ASD2315**

SCHUBERT
No. 5 in B flat, D.485
(c/w Schubert: Symphony No. 3)
   Royal Philharmonic/Sir Thomas Beecham   **ASD345/ALP1743**
No. 8 in B minor, D.759 ("Unfinished")
(c/w Brahms: Variations on a theme of Haydn)
   Philharmonia/Carlo Maria Giulini   **SAX2424/CX1778**
No. 9 in C, D.944 ("The Great ")
   Hallé/Sir John Barbirolli   **ASD/ALP2251**

SCHUMANN
No. 1 in B flat, Op. 38 ("Spring")
(c/w Schumann: Manfred Overture)
   New Philharmonia/Otto Klemperer   **SAX/CX5269**

SIBELIUS
No. 1 in E minor, Op. 39
(c/w Sibelius: Pelleas and Melisande – excerpts)
   Hallé/Sir John Barbirolli   **ASD2366**
No. 2 in D, Op. 43
(c/w Sibelius: The Swan of Tuonela)
   Hallé/Sir John Barbirolli   **ASD/ALP2308**
No. 5 in E flat, Op. 82
(c/w Sibelius: No. 7 in C, Op. 105)
   Hallé/Sir John Barbirolli   **ASD2326**

STRAVINSKY
Symphony in Three Movements
(c/w Stravinsky: Pulcinella)
   Philharmonia/Otto Klemperer   **SAX2588/CX1949**

TCHAIKOVSKY
No. 4 in F minor, Op. 36
   Philharmonia/Otto Klemperer   **SAX2494/CX1851**
Symphony No. 5 in E minor, Op. 64
   Philharmonia/Otto Klemperer   **SAX2497/CX1854**
No. 6 in B minor, Op. 74 ("Pathétique")
   London Symphony/Jascha Horenstein   **ASD2332**

VAUGHAN WILLIAMS
No. 4 in F minor
(c/w Vaughan Williams: Norfolk Rhapsody No. 1)
   New Philharmonia/Sir Adrian Boult   **ASD2375**
No. 5 in D
   Philharmonia/Sir John Barbirolli   **ASD508/ALP1957**
No. 6 in E minor
(c/w Vaughan Williams: The Lark Ascending)
   New Philharmonia/Sir Adrian Boult   **ASD2329**
Sinfonia Antartica
   Hallé/Sir John Barbirolli   **ALP1102**
A London Symphony
   Hallé/Sir John Barbirolli   **ASD2360**

WALTON
No. 1 in B flat minor
   New Philharmonia/Sir Malcolm Sargent   **ASD/ALP2299**

ORCHESTRAL

BALAKIREV

Tone Poem: Russia
Overture on Russian Themes
(c/w Borodin: Symphony No. 1)
    Philharmonia/Lovro von Matacic   XLP30107

BEETHOVEN

Egmont Overture, Op. 84
Coriolan Overture, Op. 62
(c/w Prometheus, King Stephen and the Consecration of the House Overtures)
    Philharmonia/Otto Klemperer   SAX2570/CX1330
Overtures: Leonora No. 1, Op. 138, Leonora No. 2, Op. 72 and Leonora
No. 3, Op. 72a, Fidelio, Op. 72b
    Philharmonia/Otto Klemperer   SAX2542/CX1902

BIZET

L'Arlésienne: Suites 1 and 2
(c/w Bizet: Carmen Suite)
    Royal Philharmonic and French National Radio
    Sir Thomas Beecham   HQS1108

BORODIN

Polovtsian Dances from "Prince Igor"
(c/w Borodin: "Prince Igor" – Highlights)
    Sofia National Opera Chorus and Orchestra/Jerzy Semkow ASD2345

BRAHMS

Variations on a theme of Haydn, Op. 56a
(c/w Schubert: "Unfinished" Symphony)
    Philharmonia/Carlo Maria Giulini   SAX2424/CX1778

BRITTEN

Variations and Fugue on a theme of Purcell, Op. 34 ("Young Person's
Guide to the Orchestra")
(c/w Britten: Four Sea Interludes from "Peter Grimes")
    Philharmonia/Carlo Maria Giulini   SAX2555/CX1915

DEBUSSY

Prélude à l'après-midi d'un faune
(c/w music by Berlioz, Chabrier, etc.)
    Royal Philharmonic/Sir Thomas Beecham   ASD259/ALP1533
La Mer
(c/w Nocturnes)
    Philharmonia/Carlo Maria Giulini   SAX2463/CX1818

DELIBES

Coppélia, Ballet Suite
Sylvia, Ballet Suite
    Philharmonia/Robert Irving   ASD439/ALP1869

ELGAR

Introduction and Allegro for Strings, Op. 47
(c/w Elgar: Serenade; Vaughan Williams: Tallis Fantasia and Greensleeves)
    Sinfonia of London/Sir John Barbirolli   ASD521/ALP1970
In the South, Concert Overture, Op. 50
(c/w Vaughan Williams: The Wasps Overture; Tallis Fantasia)
    Bournemouth Symphony/Constantin Silvestri   ASD2370
Pomp and Circumstance Marches Nos. 1 to 5
(c/w Elgar: Froissart; Sospiri; Elegy)
    Philharmonia and New Philharmonia/Sir John Barbirolli
                                     ASD/ALP2292

ELGAR (contd.)

"Enigma" Variations, Op. 36
(c/w Elgar: Cockaigne)
    Philharmonia/Sir John Barbirolli   **ASD548/ALP1998**
The Wand of Youth: Suites 1 and 2
(c/w Elgar: Three Bavarian Dances; Chanson de Matin, Chanson de Nuit)
    London Philharmonic/Sir Adrian Boult   **ASD2356**

GRIEG

Peer Gynt – incidental music to Ibsen's play
    Ilse Hollweg, Beecham Choral Society, Royal Philharmonic
    Sir Thomas Beecham   **ASD258/ALP1530**

HANDEL

The Water Music (edited by N. Boyling)
    Bath Festival/Yehudi Menuhin   **ASD577/ALP2028**
Music for the Royal Fireworks: Suite arr. Harty
(c/w Handel–Harty: Water Music Suite; Overture in D minor; Overture: Samson
arr. Elgar)
    Royal Philharmonic/Sir Malcolm Sargent   **ASD286/ALP1710**

HOLST

The Planets, Op. 32
    New Philharmonia/Sir Adrian Boult   **ASD/ALP2301**

MENDELSSOHN

A Midsummer Night's Dream – incidental music, Op. 61
    Philharmonia/Otto Klemperer   **SAX2393/CX1746**
The Hebrides (Fingal's Cave) Overture, Op. 26
(c/w Mendelssohn: "Scotch" Symphony)
    Philharmonia/Otto Klemperer   **SAX2342/CX1736**

MOUSSORGSKY

Pictures at an Exhibition
(c/w Respighi: Fountains of Rome)
    Royal Philharmonic/Sir Eugene Goossens   **SXLP/XLP30068**

MOZART

Serenade: Eine kleine Nachtmusik, K.525
(c/w Mozart: Symphony No. 25; Handel: Concerto Grosso Op. 6, No. 4)
    Philharmonia and New Philharmonia/Otto Klemperer   **SAX/CX5252**

PROKOFIEV

Peter and the Wolf
(c/w Saint-Saëns: Carnival of the Animals)
    Michael Flanders, Philharmonia/Efrem Kurtz   **ASD299/ALP1728**

RAVEL

Daphnis and Chloë, complete ballet
    Ambrosian Singers/New Philharmonia/Rafael Frühbeck de Burgos
Bolero   **ASD2355**
La Valse
(c/w Ravel: Rapsodie Espagnole)
    Paris Conservatoire/André Cluytens   **SAX2477/CX1833**

RIMSKY-KORSAKOV

Caprice Espagnol, Op. 34
(c/w Music by Moussorgsky and Rimsky-Korsakov)
    Royal Philharmonic/Georges Prêtre   **ASD509/ALP1958**
Scheherazade, Op. 35
    Royal Philharmonic/Sir Thomas Beecham   **ASD251/ALP1564**

SCHUMANN
Manfred Overture, Op. 115
(c/w Schumann: "Spring" Symphony)
    New Philharmonia/Otto Klemperer   **SAX/CX5269**

SIBELIUS
Finlandia, Op. 26
(c/w Sibelius: Karelia Suite; Valse Triste; Pohjola's Daughter; Lemminkäinen's Return)
    Hallé/Sir John Barbirolli   **ASD/ALP2272**
The Swan of Tuonela
(c/w Sibelius: Symphony No. 2)
    Hallé/Sir John Barbirolli   **ASD/ALP2308**

SMETANA
Má Vlast – Cycle of 6 symphonic poems: Vyšehrad; Vltava; Šárka; From Bohemia's Woods and Meadows; Tabor; Bianik
(c/w Dvořák: Symphonic Variations)
    Royal Philharmonic/Sir Malcolm Sargent   **SXLP/XLP20064/-5**

RICHARD STRAUSS
Don Juan
Till Eulenspiegel's Merry Pranks
Dance of the Seven Veils from "Salome"
    Philharmonia/Otto Klemperer   **SAX2367/CX1715**

STRAVINSKY
The Rite of Spring
(c/w Prokofiev: Classical Symphony)
    New Philharmonia/Rafael Frühbeck de Burgos   **ASD2315**

TCHAIKOVSKY
1812 Overture
(c/w Tchaikovsky: Polonaise from "Eugene Onegin"; Caprice italien)
    Bournemouth Symphony/Constantin Silvestri   **TWO139/SX6086**
Romeo and Juliet, Fantasy Overture
(c/w Tchaikovsky: Francesca da Rimini)
    Philharmonia/Carlo Maria Giulini   **SAX2483/CX1840**
Serenade in C Op. 48
(c/w Arensky: Variations on a theme by Tchaikovsky)
    London Symphony/Sir John Barbirolli   **ASD646/ALP2099**
The Nutcracker: Suite
(c/w Tchaikovsky: The Sleeping Beauty)
    Royal Philharmonic/Sir Adrian Boult   **TWO183**
Swan Lake: Ballet Suite
(c/w Tchaikovsky: The Sleeping Beauty)
    Philharmonia/Herbert von Karajan   **SAX2306/CX1065**

WAGNER
Tannhäuser Overture
(c/w Wagner: Rienzi Overture; The Flying Dutchman Overture; Lohengrin – Prelude, Act 1)
    Philharmonia/Otto Klemperer   **SAX2347/CX1697**
Siegfried Idyll
(c/w Schœnberg: Verklärte Nacht; Hindemith: Trauermusik)
    English Chamber Orchestra/Daniel Barenboim   **ASD2346**
Tristan und Isolde: Prelude and Liebestod
Lohengrin: Prelude, Act 3
Götterdämmerung: Siegfried's Funeral March
(c/w Wagner: Die Meistersinger von Nürnberg – Overture and Dance of the Apprentices; Entry of the Masters)
    Philharmonia/Otto Klemperer   **SAX2348/CX1698**

CONCERTOS

J. S. BACH
Brandenburg Concertos Nos. 1 to 3   ASD327/ALP1755
                    Nos. 4 to 6   ASD328/ALP1756
   Bath Festival/Yehudi Menuhin
Double Concerto in D minor
(c/w J. S. Bach: Violin Concertos in A minor and E)
   Yehudi Menuhin, Christian Ferras/Bath Festival   ASD346/ALP1760

BEETHOVEN
Piano Concerto No. 4 in G, Op. 58
(c/w Beethoven: Rondo in G)
   Hans Richter-Haaser/Philharmonia/Istvan Kertesz   SAX2403/CX1757
Piano Concerto No. 5 in E flat, Op. 73 ("Emperor")
(c/w Beethoven: Rondo in C)
   Hans Richter-Haaser/Philharmonia/Istvan Kertesz   SAX2422/CX1775
Violin Concerto in D, Op. 61
   Yehudi Menuhin/Philharmonia/Otto Klemperer   ASD/ALP2285

BOCCHERINI
Cello Concerto in B flat (arr. Grützmacher)
(c/w Haydn: Cello Concerto in C)
   Jacqueline du Pré/English Chamber/Daniel Barenboim   ASD2331

BRAHMS
Violin Concerto in D, Op. 77
   David Oistrakh/French National/Otto Klemperer   SAX2411/CX1765
Piano Concerto No. 1 in D minor, Op. 15
   Daniel Barenboim/New Philharmonia/Sir John Barbirolli   ASD2353
Piano Concerto No. 2 in B flat, Op. 83
   Daniel Barenboim/New Philharmonia/Sir John Barbirolli   ASD2413
Double Concerto in A minor, Op. 102
(c/w Brahms: Tragic Overture)
   David Oistrakh (violin), Pierre Fournier (cello)
   Philharmonia/Alceo Galliera   SAX2264/CX1487

CHOPIN
Piano Concerto No. 1 in E minor, Op. 11
   Maurizio Pollini/Philharmonia/Paul Kletzki   ASD370/ALP1794

DVOŘÁK
Cello Concerto in B minor, Op. 104
   Mstislav Rostropovitch/Royal Philharmonic/Sir Adrian Boult
                                       ASD358/ALP1595

ELGAR
Violin Concerto in B minor, Op. 61
   Yehudi Menuhin/New Philharmonia/Sir Adrian Boult   ASD/ALP2259
Cello Concerto in E minor, Op. 85
(c/w Sea Pictures/Janet Baker)
   Jacqueline du Pré/London Symphony/Sir John Barbirolli
                                       ASD655/ALP2106

GRIEG
Piano Concerto in A minor, Op. 16
(c/w Schumann: Concerto in A minor, Op. 54)
   Solomon/Philharmonia/Herbert Menges   ASD272/ALP1643

LISZT
Piano Concerto No. 1 in E flat
(c/w Schumann Piano Concerto)
   Annie Fischer/Philharmonia/Otto Klemperer   SAX2485/CX1842

MENDELSSOHN
Violin Concerto in E minor, Op. 64
(c/w Bruch: Violin Concerto No. 1 in G minor, Op. 26)
   Yehudi Menuhin/Philharmonia/Efrem Kurtz   **ASD334/ALP1669**

MOZART
Piano Concerto No. 23 in A, K.488
(c/w Piano Concerto No. 20 D minor, K.466)
   Daniel Barenboim/English Chamber   **ASD2318**
Piano Concerto No. 24 in C minor, K.491
(c/w Mozart: Piano Concerto No. 27, B flat K.595)
   Annie Fischer/New Philharmonia/Efrem Kurtz   **SAX5287**
Clarinet Concerto in A, K.622
(c/w Mozart: Bassoon Concerto K.191)
   Jack Brymer/Royal Philharmonic/Sir Thomas Beecham
         ASD344/ALP1768

Horn Concertos Nos. 1–4
   Dennis Brain/Philharmonia/Herbert von Karajan   **CX1140**

Violin Concertos No. 4 in D, K.218 and No. 5 in A, K.219 ("Turkish")
   Nathan Milstein/Philharmonia   **SAX/CX5254**
Sinfonia Concertante in E flat, K.364
(c/w Haydn: Violin Concerto in C)
   Yehudi Menuhin (violin) Rudolf Barshai (viola)/Bath Festival
         ASD567/ALP2017

RACHMANINOV
Piano Concerto No. 2 in C minor, Op. 18
(c/w Rachmaninov: Rhapsody on a theme of Paganini)
   Agustin Anievas/New Philharmonia/Moshe Atzmon   **ASD2361**

TCHAIKOVSKY
Piano Concerto No. 1 in B flat minor, Op. 23
(c/w Franck: Symphonic Variations)
   John Ogdon/Philharmonia/Sir John Barbirolli   **ASD542/ALP1991**
Violin Concerto in D, Op. 35
(c/w Tchaikovsky: Meditation)
   Leonid Kogan/Paris Conservatoire/Constantin Silvestri
         SAX2323/CX1711

MUSIC OF THE BAROQUE PERIOD

ALBINONI
Five Oboe Concertos
   Pierre Pierlot/"Antiqua Musica" Chamber Orchestra
   Jacques Roussel   **HQS/HQM1036**

GABRIELI
Music for choir, brass and string ensembles by Andrea and Giovanni Gabrieli
   Ambrosian Singers/Instrumental Ensembles/Denis Stevens
         HQS1093

MONTEVERDI
Madrigals
   April Cantelo, Helen Watts, Robert Tear, etc./members of the English
   Chamber Orchestra/Raymond Leppard   **HQS1102**

VIVALDI
Four Concertos for Two Orchestras
   Les Solistes de Bruxelles/I Solisti di Milano/Angelo Ephrikian
         HQS/HQM1060

EARLY GERMAN OPERA FROM THE GOOSEMARKET
Excerpts from Boris Goudenow (Mattheson), Pimpinone (Telemann),
Almira (Handel), Croesus (Keiser)
  Lisa Otto, Hermann Prey, Theo Adam/Berlin Philharmonic/
  Wilhelm Brückner-Rüggeberg   **HQS/HQM1037**

EVENING CONCERT AT ST. MARIEN, LÜBECK
Music by Tunder, Buxtehude and Nicolaus Bruhns
  Edith Mathis, Hermann Prey/Windsbach Boys' Choir/Hans Thamm
          HQS/HQM1038

INSTRUMENTAL AND CHAMBER MUSIC

J. S. BACH

The Well-Tempered Clavier, Books 1 and 2
(c/w J. S. Bach: Chromatic Fantasia; Italian Concerto)
  Helmut Walcha   **HQS/HQM1042–3, HQS/HQM1065–67**
Goldberg Variations
(c/w J. S. Bach: 2 and 3 Part Inventions)
  Helmut Walcha   **HQS1129–30**
Passacaglia and Fugue in C minor, BWV.582
(c/w J. S. Bach: Organ works including Toccata and Fugue in D minor)
  Fernando Germani   **CSD1318/CLP1380**

BEETHOVEN

Piano Sonatas No. 8 in C minor, Op. 13 ("Pathétique")
           No. 14 in C sharp minor, Op. 27, No. 2 ("Moonlight")
           No. 23 in F minor, Op. 57 ("Appassionata")
  Daniel Barenboim   **HQS/HQM1076**
Piano Sonatas No. 19 in G minor, Op. 49, No. 1
           No. 26 in E flat, Op. 81a ("Les Adieux")
           No. 32 in C minor, Op. 111
  Daniel Barenboim   **HQS/HQM1088**
Violin Sonatas No. 5 in F, Op. 24 ("Spring")
           No. 9 in A, Op. 47 ("Kreutzer")
  Yehudi Menuhin and Hephzibah Menuhin   **ASD389/ALP1739**
Cello Sonatas No. 3 in A, Op. 69
           No. 5 in D, Op. 102, No. 2
  Jacqueline du Pré and Stephen Bishop   **HQS/HQM1029**

BRAHMS

Clarinet Quintet in B minor, Op. 115
  Gervase de Peyer and the Melos Ensemble   **ASD620/ALP2072**
Horn Trio in E flat, Op. 40
(c/w Brahms: Piano Trio No. 2)
  Alan Civil, Yehudi Menuhin, Hephzibah Menuhin,   **ASD2354**
Sextet No. 1 in B flat major, Op. 18
  Yehudi Menuhin, Robert Masters, Cecil Aronowitz, Ernst Wallfisch,
  Maurice Gendron and Derek Simpson   **ASD587/ALP2038**

CHOPIN

Etudes: Opp. 10 and 25
  Agustin Anievas   **HQS/HQM1058**
Preludes 1–24, Op. 28, C sharp minor, Op. 45 and A flat, Op. posth.
  Rafael Orozco   **HQS1125**
Valses Nos. 1–14
  Malcuzynski   **SAX2332/CX1685**

COUPERIN

6me Ordre in B flat and 22me Ordre in D
(c/w Handel: Harpsichord music)
  George Malcolm   **HQS/HQM1085**

HANDEL
Prelude, Air and Variations in B flat
Fantasia in C
Minuet in G minor
Chaconne and 21 Variations in G
(c/w Couperin: Harpsichord music)
   George Malcolm   **HQS/HQM1085**

MOZART
Piano Quartet No. 1 in G minor, K.478
(c/w Mozart: Piano Quartet No. 2 in E flat, K.493)
   Fou Ts'ong, Yehudi Menuhin, Walter Gerhardt, Gaspar Cassado
                              ASD2319

Clarinet Quintet in A, K.581
(c/w Mozart: Trio, K.498)
   Gervase de Peyer and members of the Melos Ensemble
                            ASD605/ALP2056

String Quintets in G minor, K.516 and D K.593
   Heutling Quartet with Heinz-Otto Graf (viola)   **HQS1120**

RAVEL
Introduction and Allegro (Septet)
(c/w harp music by Debussy and Pierné)
   Annie Challan (harp)/members of the Paris Conservatoire Orchestra
   André Cluytens   **SCX3568/SX1768**

SCHUBERT
Quintet in A, D.667 ("Trout")
(c/w Schubert: Adagio and Rondo Concertante)
   Lamar Crowson and the Melos Ensemble   **ASD2328**

SCHUMANN
Kinderszenen (Scenes from Childhood), Op. 15
(c/w Schumann: Kreisleriana, Op. 16)
   Annie Fischer   **SAX2583/CX1944**

TCHAIKOVSKY
String Quartet No. 1 in D, Op. 11
(c/w Schumann: Piano Quintet)
   Smetana Quartet   **ASD2386**

VOCAL
BRAHMS
Alto Rhapsody
(c/w Songs by Mahler and Wagner)
   Christa Ludwig/Philharmonia/Otto Klemperer   **ASD2391**
Deutsche Volkslieder
   Elisabeth Schwarzkopf/Dietrich Fischer-Dieskau/Gerald Moore
                             SAN/AN163–4

FALLA
Seven Popular Spanish Songs
(c/w Songs by Ravel, Debussy, etc.)
   Victoria de los Angeles and Gonzalo Soriano   **ASD/ALP2260**

MAHLER
Kindertotenlieder
(c/w Mahler: Lieder eines fahrenden gesellen etc.)
   Janet Baker/Hallé/Sir John Barbirolli   **ASD2338**

MOUSSORGSKY
The Nursery; Sunless; Songs and Dances of Death
   Boris Christoff and Alexandre Labinsky
   French National Radio/Georges Tzipine   **ALP2310**

PURCELL

Sleep, Adam, Sleep; Lord, what is man?
(c/w Songs by English composers 1597–1961)
    Janet Baker and Gerald Moore and instrumental acc.   **HQS1091**

SCHUBERT

Die schöne Müllerin, D.795
    Dietrich Fischer-Dieskau and Gerald Moore   **ASD481/ALP1913**
Winterreisse, D.911   **ASDS551/ASD552**
    Dietrich Fischer-Dieskau and Gerald Moore   **ALPS2001/ALP2002**
Popular Schubert songs including
Du bist die Ruh', Heidenröslein, Horch, horch die Lerch, Die Forelle, etc.
    Dietrich Fischer-Dieskau and Gerald Moore   **ASD/ALP2263**

SCHUMANN

Dichterliebe, Op. 48
    Hermann Prey and Karl Engel   **SAX2567/CX1927**
Liederkreis, Op. 39 and other Eichendorff songs
    Dietrich Fischer-Dieskau and Gerald Moore   **ASD650/ALP2103**

CHORAL MUSIC

J. S. BACH

Mass in B minor
    Agnes Giebel, Janet Baker, Nicolai Gedda, Hermann Prey, Franz Crass
    BBC Chorus/New Philharmonia/Otto Klemperer   **SAN195-7**
St. Matthew Passion
    Peter Pears, Elisabeth Schwarzkopf, Christa Ludwig/Philharmonia
    Orchestra and Choir/Otto Klemperer
                  SAXS2446, SAX2447-50/CXS1799, CX1800-3

BEETHOVEN

Missa Solemnis in D, Op. 123
    Elisabeth Söderström, Marga Höffgen, Waldemar Kmentt, Martti
    Talvela/New Philharmonia Chorus and Orchestra/Otto Klemperer
                   SAN/AN165-6

BRAHMS

German Requiem, Op. 45
    Elisabeth Schwarzkopf, Dietrich Fischer-Dieskau/Philharmonia Orch-
    estra and Chorus/Otto Klemperer
               SAXS2430, SAX2431/CXS1781, CX1782

ELGAR

The Dream of Gerontius, Op. 38
    Richard Lewis, Janet Baker, Kim Borg, Ambrosian Singers/Sheffield
    Philharmonic and Hallé Choirs/Hallé/Sir John Barbirolli
                  ASD648-9/ALP2101-2

FAURÉ

Requiem, Op. 48
(c/w Fauré: Pavane)
    Robert Chilcott, John Carol Case, King's College Choir, Cambridge
    New Philharmonia/David Willcocks   **ASD2358**

HANDEL

Messiah (ed. Basil Lam)
    Elizabeth Harwood, Janet Baker, Paul Esswood, Robert Tear, Raimund
    Herincx, Ambrosian Singers/English Chamber/Charles Mackerras
                  HQS/HQM1052-4

MENDELSSOHN

Elijah
    Gwyneth Jones, Janet Baker, Nicolai Gedda, Dietrich Fischer-Dieskau
    New Philharmonia Chorus and Orchestra/Rafael Frühbeck de Burgos
                  SAN212-4

MOZART

Requiem, K.626
  Edith Mathis, Grace Bumbry, George Shirley, Marius Rintzler/New
  Philharmonia Chorus and Orchestra/Rafael Frühbeck de Burgos
  SAN193

ORFF

Carmina Burana
  Lucia Popp, Gerhard Unger, Raymond Wolansky, John Noble/New
  Philharmonia Chorus and Orchestra/Rafael Frühbeck de Burgos
  SAN/AN162

PARRY

Blest Pair of Sirens
(c/w Elgar: The Music Makers)
  London Philharmonic Choir and Orchestra/Sir Adrian Boult
  ASD/ALP2311

VERDI

Requiem
  Elisabeth Schwarzkopf, Christa Ludwig, Nicolai Gedda, Nicolai
  Ghiaurov/Philharmonia Chorus and Orchestra/Carlo Maria Giulini
  SAN/AN133–4

WALTON

Belshazzar's Feast
(c/w Walton: Partita)
  Donald Bell/Philharmonia Chorus and Orchestra/Sir William Walton
  SAX2319/CX1679

OPERA
BEETHOVEN

Fidelio
  Christa Ludwig, Jon Vickers, Gottlob Frick/Philharmonia Chorus and
  Orchestra/Otto Klemperer   SAX2451–3/CX1804–6

BIZET

Carmen
  Victoria de los Angeles, Nicolai Gedda, Ernest Blanc/French National
  Radio Orchestra and Chorus/Sir Thomas Beecham
  ASD331–3/ALP1762–4

BORODIN

Prince Igor – Highlights
  Boris Christoff/Sofia National Opera/Jerzy Semkow   ASD2345

DONIZETTI

Lucia di Lammermoor
  Maria Callas, Ferruccio Tagliavini, Piero Cappuccillo, Bernard Ladysz
  Philharmonia Orchestra and Chorus/Tullio Serafin
  SAX2316–7/CX1723–4

GLUCK

Orfeo ed Euridice – Highlights
  Grace Bumbry, Anneliese Rothenberger/Leipzig Radio Chorus/Leipzig
  Gewandhaus Orchestra/Vaclav Neumann   ASD2378

GOUNOD

Faust
  Victoria de los Angeles, Rita Gorr, Nicolai Gedda, Boris Christoff/Paris
  Opera Orchestra and Chorus/André Cluytens   ASD307–10/ALP1721–4

LEHÁR

The Merry Widow
  Elisabeth Schwarzkopf, Eberhard Wächter, Nicolai Gedda, Hanny
  Steffek/Philharmonia Chorus and Orchestra/Lovro von Matacic
  SAN/AN101–2

MASCAGNI
Cavalleria Rusticana (Side 4 - Operatic excerpts by Mascagni)
Victoria de los Angeles, Franco Corelli/Rome Opera House Orchestra
and Chorus/Gabriele Santini   SAN/AN108-9

MOZART
Don Giovanni
Nicolai Ghiaurov, Walter Berry, Nicolai Gedda, Christa Ludwig, Claire
Watson, Mirella Freni/New Philharmonia Orchestra and Chorus/Otto
Klemperer   SAN/AN172-5

The Marriage of Figaro
Elisabeth Schwarzkopf, Anna Moffo, Eberhard Wächter, Giuseppe
Taddei, Ivo Vinco/Philharmonia Orchestra and Chorus/Carlo Maria
Giulini   SAX2381-4/CX1732-5

The Magic Flute
Lucia Popp, Gundula Janowitz, Elisabeth Schwarzkopf, Nicolai Gedda,
Walter Berry, Franz Crass/Philharmonia Orchestra and Chorus/Otto
Klemperer   SAN/AN137-9

PUCCINI
La Bohème
Mirella Freni, Nicolai Gedda/Rome Opera House Orchestra and Chorus
Thomas Schippers   SAN/AN131-2

Madama Butterfly
Renata Scotto, Carlo Bergonzi, Rolando Panerai/Rome Opera House
Orchestra and Chorus/Sir John Barbirolli   SAN184-6

Tosca
Maria Callas, Carlo Bergonzi, Tito Gobbi/Paris Conservatoire Orchestra
and Paris Opera Chorus/Georges Prêtre   SAN/AN149-50

PURCELL
Dido and Aeneas
Victoria de los Angeles, Heather Harper, Peter Glossop/Ambrosian
Singers/English Chamber Orchestra/Sir John Barbirolli SAN/AN169

ROSSINI
The Barber of Seville
Victoria de los Angeles, Luigi Alva, Sesto Bruscantini, Ian Wallace
Glyndebourne Festival Chorus/Royal Philharmonic/Vittorio Gui
            SAN/AN114-6

RICHARD STRAUSS
Der Rosenkavalier
Elisabeth Schwarzkopf, Teresa Stich Randall, Christa Ludwig, Nicolai
Gedda, Eberhard Wächter, Otto Edelmann/Philharmonia Orchestra and
Chorus/Herbert von Karajan   SAX2269-72/CX1492-5

VERDI
Aida
Birgit Nilsson, Franco Corelli, Grace Bumbry/Rome Opera House Orch-
estra and Chorus/Zubin Mehta   SAN189-91

La Traviata
Victoria de los Angeles, Carlo del Monte, Mario Sereni/Rome Opera
House Orchestra and Chorus/Tullio Serafin   ASD359-61/ALP1780-2

WAGNER
The Mastersingers of Nuremburg
Elisabeth Grümmer, Rudolf Schock, Ferdinand Frantz, Gottlob Frick
Berlin Philharmonic Orchestra with Chorus/Rudolf Kempe HQM1094-8

WEBER
Der Freischütz
Elisabeth Grümmer, Rudolf Schock, Hermann Prey, Gottlob Frick
Berlin Municipal Opera Chorus/Berlin Philharmonic/Joseph Keilberth
            HQS/HQM1031-2

INDEX

190

192